FEMALE GENITAL CUTTING

Female Genital Cutting

*Cultural Conflict
in the Global Community*

. . . .

ELIZABETH HEGER BOYLE

The Johns Hopkins University Press
Baltimore and London

© 2002 The Johns Hopkins University Press
All rights reserved. Published 2002
Printed in the United States of America on acid-free paper

Johns Hopkins Paperbacks edition, 2005
9 8 7 6 5 4 3 2 1

The Johns Hopkins University Press
2715 North Charles Street
Baltimore, Maryland 21218-4363
www.press.jhu.edu

The Library of Congress has catalogued the hardcover edition of this book as follows:
Boyle, Elizabeth Heger, 1962–
Female genital cutting : cultural conflict in the global community /
Elizabeth Heger Boyle.
p. cm.
Includes bibliographical references and index.
ISBN 0-8018-7063-1 (hardcover : alk. paper)
1. Female circumcision — Prevention.   2. Female circumcision —
Government policy.   3. Female circumcision — Religious aspects.
4. World health.   I. Title.
GN484 .B69   2002
392.1—dc21
2001008638

ISBN 0-8018-8263-X (pbk.: alk. paper)

A catalog record for this book is available from the British Library.

To Matt, Aidan, and Claire,
with love

CONTENTS

· ·

Last spring I was flipping through television stations and came across the show *48 Hours*. The title of the segment I caught was "Not Tonight Dear: Low Sex Drive in Women Can Be Treated with Hormone Therapy If Properly Diagnosed."[1] The show began with interviews of two couples with small children. With both of the couples, the women had become less interested in sex after having babies. One woman confided: "I have no sexual drive all of a sudden. My libido is—is disappearing." The other woman stated, "I don't desire it at all anymore, at all. It's—it's weird because before I did, and now I don't." The reporter then noted that experts estimate that nearly one-half of all American women have "sexual dysfunction." These women's most common complaint is a loss of desire, which may be linked to a reduction in testosterone during pregnancy. The reporter then explained how hormone medication could cure the problem: "She'll have a choice in how she takes her hormone therapy—a pill, patch, or creams. To prevent side effects, like unwanted hair, the dosage is adjusted."

As I watched, I was struck by how the show turned a naturally occurring period in a woman's life into an illness. If many women have a reduced sex drive right after giving birth, then perhaps it is normal and not pathological to have a reduced sex drive right after giving birth. Even if they do not resort to medication, the presumption that something is wrong is very stressful for women. For example, during the program, a tearful woman confessed: "At 3:00 in the afternoon I'd be thinking, 'He's coming home in a couple of hours. It has—it's been a w—— you know, two weeks,' you know, and I would just try to, you know, mentally prepare for it." The message of the program was that the reduction in sex drive, whether psychological or physical in origin, was a "problem." The show clearly assumed that great sex all the time was the natural state of affairs, even though the show's own evidence refuted that presumption.

If the expectation for great sex is too high in the United States, the opposite expectation might be said to exist in other parts of the world. In many of the regions I will be discussing in this book, enjoying sex (at least until recently) was viewed as superfluous, childish, or even dangerous for women. There was an assumption that, without intervention, women could enjoy sex too much and be unable to control their desires. This could lead women to have premarital sex, engage in affairs, and perhaps even neglect their children. In these communities, female genital cutting might be viewed as useful or necessary to help women avoid these problems. While in the United States couples seek treatment to *increase* women's sexual desire, in these other parts of the world there are surgeries specifically designed to *reduce* women's sexual desire.

In both cases, women's sex drive is something that "needs" to be fixed. In both cases, men are the presumptive beneficiaries of the intervention. In both cases, women are made to feel ashamed and uncomfortable with their sexuality.

Currently, female genital cutting is more serious than the medicalization of postpartum sexuality. In the cultures where it occurs, female genital cutting tends to be widespread, involves children, can result in serious health consequences, and permanently affects a woman's sexuality. I use the *48 Hours* example not to trivialize female genital cutting but to illustrate that sex is much more than a physical act driven by "natural" biological processes. Sex is a social phenomenon, and that makes it a mysterious interaction everywhere. No culture has a "perfect" view of how sex fits into society, how much sex is normal, or even what sex really is.

In some cultures and communities, the point of sex is to have children. When Lori Leonard asked a woman in the town of Myabé in southern Chad, "How is sex after circumcision?" the woman responded, "Both circumcised and uncircumcised women give birth so I don't see the difference" (Leonard 2000, 220). For this woman, having sex frequently or deriving sexual pleasure may take a second-ary role to childrearing.

This is very different from the United States, where sex is often about individual fulfillment and the relationship between sexual part-ners. The explicit message of the *48 Hours* show was that something is wrong with a woman whose interest in her newborn baby outweighs her interest in sexual relations with her spouse. What is problematized as a "lack of sexual desire" by the show could be seen as a good thing and labeled "rarely sexually frustrated." The true problem is not the woman's lack of sexual desire but the *mismatch* in the partners' level of sexual desire.

I raise these contrasting examples to forestall a problem common to research on female genital cutting: ethnocentrism. Improving the lot of women means not only eradicating the practice of female geni-tal cutting but also critically assessing the social construction of sex and the family in multiple contexts. The key to overcoming ethno-centrism is recognizing that cultural learning should not be a one-sided phenomenon. All cultures of the world can learn from all other cultures. This is true *even* in the study of a practice as condemned as female genital cutting.

There are many individuals who made this book possible. The first group includes my African colleagues, students, and friends (these are overlapping categories!) who shared their knowledge with me, especially Professor John Arthur, Lucy Jalong'a, Switbert Kamazima, Colman Titus Msoka, Patricia Neema, and Fortunata Songora. These individuals provided important "reality checks" on my characteriza-tions of social and political circumstances. However, I take full re-sponsibility for any errors in the current text. If they exist, they will arise in sections about which I did not consult with these individuals.

Second, over the years, a cadre of enthusiastic research assistants and article coauthors have provided both intellectual and motiva-tional support for this project: Kristin Carbone, Mayra Gómez, An-drea Hoeschen, Dongxiao Liu, Barb McMorris, Gail Foss, Sharon Preves, Fortunata Songora, and Hui Niu Wilcox. Various combina-tions of the ten of us have published articles in *Law & Society Review*,

Sociological Quarterly, International Sociology, and *Social Problems,* with additional articles under review. It has been a true pleasure working with each of them.

Many individuals provided critical feedback as this project developed, often challenging some or all of my arguments. Dealing with their ideas forced me to clarify my own. I am therefore deeply appreciative to the graduate students and faculty in the Sociology Department at the University of Minnesota, especially Ron Aminzade, Ron Anderson, Jeff Broadbent, Sara Darrow, Katja Guenther, Doug Hartmann, Ann Hironaka, Candace Kruttschnitt, Eric Larson, Karen Lutfey, Carl Malmquist, Jeylan Mortimer, Joachim Savelsberg, Evan Schofer, and Chris Uggen.

Outside of the Sociology Department, a number of other lively communities also provided intellectual support, including the Interdisciplinary Center for the Study of Global Change/John D. and Catherine T. MacArthur consortium, the Hubert H. Humphrey Center's Women and Public Policy Reading Group, the Center for Advanced Feminist Studies, and faculty at the College of Law who thoughtfully invited me to present my ideas during a "works in progress" session. Individuals in those groups include Louis Bickford, Carolyn Chalmers, Carol Chomsky, Laura Cooper, Lisa Disch, Bud Duvall, Allen Isaacman, Stanlie James, Sally Kenney, Kathryn Sikkink, Tom Sullivan, Karen Brown Thompson, David Trubeck, and Barbara Welke.

I am deeply indebted to editors Saïd Amir Arjomand, Kevin Leicht, Susan Silbey, David Smith, and a number of anonymous reviewers who provided essential feedback on many of the ideas in this book. I would also like to thank Jeannine Bell, Elisabeth Dahl, Frank Dobbin, Wendy Espeland, David Frank, John Meyer, Leslye Obiora, Winnie Poster, Abigail Saguy, Carroll Seron, and Erica Sussman for their thoughtful comments at critical moments.

In addition to the support of these individuals, I have also been fortunate to receive much-needed funding for this project. The University of Minnesota provided seed money through its Grant-in-Aid of Research program and through its Life Course Center, and the Ronald J. McNair Summer Fellowship program provided assistance from Angela Heffernan, Joyce Bell, and Lauren Lucia. The National Science Foundation provided two years of support through its Professional Opportunities for Women in Research and Education program. Without the generous support of these institutions, this book would not have been written.

Finally, many thanks to my sister Teresa Heger, who pored over every page of the manuscript, often more than once, making detailed comments on clarity and grammar, and to Matt, Aidan, and Claire, who spent many evenings and weekends on their own so that I could put this book together.

FEMALE GENITAL CUTTING

ONE

. . . .

Introduction

Virtually every ethnography and report states that FGM [female genital mutilation] is defended and transmitted by the women. The mothers who have this done to their daughters love their children and want the best for them.
— *Gerry Mackie, "Ending Footbinding and Infibulation," 1996*

Female genital cutting (FGC) is an issue that touches on many of the complexities of politics in the modern international system. It sparks debate over gender equality, cultural autonomy, and human rights and has lead to charges of postcolonial imperialism. It has been the object of international mobilization since the late 1970s, and its eradication is an international goal. State responses to FGC are therefore an important illustration of how policymaking and resistance play out in the context of global cultural conflict.

Indeed, one of the clearest implications of the controversy over FGC is that cultural conflict *is* global. In the modern world, activists and policymakers do not simply identify and correct problems in their own neighborhood, city, or nation. They also address problems in other parts of the world. They align themselves with international organizations and circulate their messages around the globe. Certain principles are assumed to be universal: the world will be flawed until they are fully implemented everywhere. Thus, governments in the modern world take action with many principles and pressure groups in mind, acting in response to pressure that extends well beyond the territorial boundaries of their countries.

As a result, even in countries where nearly all families engage in FGC, states uniformly oppose it. Because state actors in these countries must appeal to the international community as much as to their local populations, they find themselves caught between contradictory perspectives toward FGC. These contradictions and their implications frame the inquiry of this book. To date, nearly all research on FGC has focused on the practice itself. I build on that research by pulling back the lens to consider the broader global context of FGC—international activism, national policymaking, *and* individual attitudes and beliefs about the practice.

Egypt is one nation caught between contradictory perspectives toward FGC. The Egyptian case highlights the fact that national policymaking does not simply mirror local values or conflicts. Both Muslims and Coptic Christians circumcise their daughters in Egypt. Although there are opponents to FGC in the country, the practice has been the norm there. Two ethnographers provide this context: "In the rural Egyptian hamlet where we have conducted fieldwork some women were not familiar with groups that did not circumcise their girls. When they learned that the female researcher was not circumcised, their response was disgust mixed with joking laughter. They wondered how she could have thus gotten married and questioned how her mother could have neglected such an important part of her preparation for womanhood. It was clearly unthinkable to them for a woman not to be circumcised" (Lane and Rubinstein 1996, 35; see also Messing 1980). *Failing* to circumcise one's daughters—at least until recently—was tantamount to child neglect in some Egyptian communities. Indeed, a 1996 survey determined that 97 percent of married Egyptian women aged 15 to 49 had been circumcised (Carr 1997). If state policymaking reflected local values, based on this background, one would expect Egyptian policies to encourage FGC or perhaps ensure the safe implementation of the practice. They would not ban FGC. But this is precisely the end result of Egypt's contested political process. Its ban on FGC stands in stark contrast to the attitudes of a large portion of Egyptian citizens. Initially, the state was hesitant to publicly address FGC (United Nations 1983, 1987, 1989). When international pressure to eradicate the practice mounted, Egyptian authorities were initially able to evade it. Egypt ratified the Convention for the Elimination of All Forms of Discrimination against Women (CEDAW) in 1981, which obligated it to file periodic reports on its progress toward gender equity. Egypt did not mention FGC in either of its first two reports. In response to questions from the CEDAW committee in 1990, Egypt's representative implied that FGC was uncommon in Egypt and was "gradually dying out" (United Nations 1990, 73). By 1994, however, Egypt was forced to take a position on FGC. In that year, CNN broadcast live the circumcision of a ten-year-old girl in Cairo while the city hosted an international population conference. A group of American dignitaries met with Egyptian president Hosni Mubarak immediately after the filming. According to Representative Constance Morella (Republican-Maryland), "I asked him about female genital mutilation, and he said that it does not happen, that it's not legal in Egypt. I said that [the law] must not be enforced . . . that I'd seen the CNN film. [Mubarak] said it's hard to get rid of the practice, but he said he didn't think it was happening any more in Egypt."[1] The timing of the telecast maximized international attention, and public outrage soon followed.

Newspaper reports from all over the world disparaged the practice and the Egyptian government for its inaction.[2] Many individuals, even some who had never been to Egypt and were unlikely to ever meet a circumcised woman, felt a moral obligation to act. For example, the film spurred Senator Henry Reid (Democrat-Nevada) to fight the practice (Dillon 2000). After seeing the film, Senator Reid decided to cosponsor a bill that would link U.S. foreign aid to FGC eradication efforts in countries where the practice occurred. In addition, the CNN filming had a profound effect internationally. The strongest language opposing FGC in the history of the U.N. system emanated from the Cairo population conference (Smith 1995).

Swept up in the international uproar but still immersed in a national culture that generally supported FGC, the Egyptian government floundered. The state's immediate response to the international attention was to arrest the freelance television producer who arranged the filming, accusing him of damaging Egypt's reputation.[3] When this action met with international criticism, Egypt released the producer, arrested the circumcisor, and pledged to pass a law banning FGC.[4]

The controversy was far from over. One of the most prominent Islamic clerics in the country, Sheikh Gad el-Haqq, issued a religious decree (*fatwa*) stating that FGC, although not required by Islam, was a religious ritual and an honorable deed for women. The *fatwa* recommended that local clerics encourage families to circumcise their daughters, just as they encourage individuals to pray.[5] Formal legislation was further impeded when a task force formed by the health minister denounced the idea of criminalizing FGC (Dillon 2000). A prominent FGC opponent in Egypt summarized this perspective: "For us, the struggle against FGM involves promoting the welfare of women and their right to take full control of their lives, not conducting a battle against women who circumcise their daughters" (Seif El Dawla 1999, 134).[6]

When it became clear that the Egyptian parliament was unwilling to entertain a law against FGC, President Mubarak dealt with the problem administratively.[7] His health minister extended a 1959 health decree to ban FGC in public hospitals. This did not last long. Sheikh Gad el-Haqq's criticism of the hospital ban led the Egyptian health minister to establish a compromise policy of setting aside one day a week to perform circumcisions in public hospitals. The health minister told reporters that if people were allowed to come to hospitals, they would be convinced by doctors that FGC is unwise and "go back home without insisting on the circumcision."[8]

Although the health minister's effort pacified Islamic fundamentalists, it outraged activists opposed to the practice. The Egyptian Organization for Human Rights sued Sheikh Gad el-Haqq, claiming $150,000 for damages caused by his *fatwa*. The group claimed that Gad el-Haqq was encouraging the government to execute activists opposed to the practice.[9] The suit also charged Gad el-Haqq with misrepresenting the sayings of the Prophet Mohammed by equating the circumcision of girls with that of boys.[10] Eventually, a court dismissed the suit, ruling that the members of the Egyptian Organization for Human Rights had no standing.

Five months after the health minister's compromise position was announced, another human rights group, Equality Now, disputed his claim of reducing FGC. The group argued that hospitals were performing circumcisions daily instead of once a week, that doctors were competing for opportunities to perform the procedure because of the fees involved, and that no advisory committees were present to dissuade parents against the practice.[11] That same month, hospitals were informed privately that they were to refuse to circumcise any more girls.[12]

Around the same time, the United States passed the legislation linking foreign aid to anti-FGC policies. Under Senator Reid's bill, cosponsored by Senator Patricia Schroeder (Democrat-Colorado), states in countries where FGC occurred would have to develop policies to eliminate the practice or face reductions in foreign aid from the International Monetary Fund and the World Bank. Around the same time, Macro International released its findings that 97 percent of Egyptian women had been circumcised. According to one researcher involved in the administration of the survey, "The Egyptians thought this was a dying custom and . . . this was much, much higher than they had expected."[13] Faced with nearly irrefutable evidence that FGC was persisting, the Egyptian health minister reversed his position again and forbade FGC in any government medical facility. Although representatives of Sheikh Gad el-Haqq challenged the new health ministry decree in court, ultimately the highest Egyptian court found in favor of the health minister. The Egyptian government has also publicly announced its commitment to eradication efforts: "The state is tireless in its efforts to eradicate female circumcision, by extending education, combating illiteracy and directing the media to draw attention to the damaging effects of the practice" (United Nations 1996, x). When Egypt found itself caught between international approbation and local cultural assumptions, in the end it succumbed to international pressure—at least formally. The long-term effect of Egypt's new policies has yet to be determined.

Theoretical Background

There are two very different perspectives on globalization. One group of theories sees globalization as a phenomenon that occurs from the ground up: Cultural change comes about as individuals are exposed to the ideas of a vast variety of cultures and, peacefully or through conflict, sort out which mix of cultural values will govern future action. A contrasting theory that has become increasingly important in the social sciences sees globalization as a top-down process. This theory is sociological neoinstitutionalism (see Frank, Schofer, and

Hironaka 2000; Boyle and Meyer 1998; Meyer et al. 1997; Powell and DiMaggio 1991; Meyer, Boli, and Thomas 1987). According to this perspective, historically derived "realities" are institutionalized in the international community and shape action and beliefs around the world. The consequence is that individuals and organizations aspire (or know they ought to aspire) to a standard set of ideals. The focus, then, is on homogenizing influences in the modern world.

Neoinstitutional theory is a contrast to traditional social science theories that often miss the tremendous amount of conformity that characterizes global reform by assuming the naturalness of institutionalized principles. Taking the principles themselves for granted, proponents of these theories see a need to explain deviation from the principles. For example, proponents of these theories might pose the question "Why hasn't China achieved gender equality?" This question, typical of such theorists, fails to acknowledge that the assumption—gender equality is a good thing—is itself a monumental global accomplishment. Only a century ago, public consensus over such an aspiration would have been inconceivable. For example, as recently as 1929, the British legal system was still debating whether the term "person" included women (Berkovitch 1999, 1), and as recently as 1970, women could not vote in Switzerland (Ramirez, Soysal, and Shanahan 1997). There are a vast number of other historical examples that suggest the idea of gender equality would have been difficult to even *formulate,* let alone agree upon, one hundred years ago. The criticism against traditional theories is that they must delve more deeply into the social construction of those assumptions that guide the global community.

On the other hand, neoinstitutionalism also has shortcomings. Neoinstitutionalists tend to bracket what actually happens on the ground, while other theoretical perspectives tend to have exactly the opposite problem. Neoinstitutionalists emphasize that over long periods of time reform does tend to occur, because individuals, like nation-states, are part of the institutionalized structures and beliefs. Thus, neoinstitutionalists focus on policy aspirations and rarely take differences in individual reactions to policies seriously (but see Brinton and Nee 1998). "Decoupling," or a lack of connection between policy and action, is natural because policies reflect what the world *ought* to be rather than what it *is*.

In fact, it is a mistake to take either the institutionalized principles or decoupling from them for granted. It is time for a theoretical perspective that critically evaluates *both* the reality of the institutionalized principles *and* real actions on the ground. In other words, social science needs to examine the interaction of homogeneous global policy with heterogeneous local actions. As Robertson notes, the true problem is "spelling out the ways in which homogenizing and heterogenizing tendencies are mutually implicative" (1995, 27). In this way, systematic connections between the two "spheres of reality" can be bridged.

Throughout this book, I develop three arguments. First, I argue that global institutionalized principles drive national policies as much as local constituents do. For example, the Egyptian case challenges the assumption underlying most current models of policymaking: that politics is primarily a local phenomenon. Nation-states do not necessarily develop policies autonomously. Local elections, local social movements, and local political coalitions may not be the primary driving forces behind policy reform. Nations are also responding to global discourse and sometimes direct international pressure. Nation-states are linked not only to their local populations but also to a global community of nation-states. Building on a long literature in sociological neoinstitutionalism, I show that anti-FGC policies diffused rapidly in the 1990s (chapter 5). The nature of those policies suggests that local factors were less important than global norms in spurring and shaping reform.

Second, I contend that particular institutions affect particular groups in different but predictable ways. In an important article, Jepperson (1991) argued that institutions and institutionalization vary across places and levels. For example, one might claim that voting is institutionalized in the United States but not in Haiti. Voting is embedded in many supportive and reproducing practices in the United States and is not highly dependent on repeated international intervention for its deployment. The same is not necessarily true of voting in Haiti. Thus, a practice may be institutionalized in one location but not in another. Perspective is also important in understanding institutions. The stock market is an institution to most Americans. To an investment banker, however, the overarching concept "stock market" may not be very meaningful; such a person may consciously reflect on each of the complex components that constitute the stock market. Thus, processes institutionalized for some are not necessarily taken for granted by all.

Building on this theme, I argue that the structural location of different groups in the international system affects their enactment of institutions in predictable ways. I demonstrate that the institutionalized precept of sovereign autonomy interacted with the structural location of different actors to uniquely affect the anti-FGC strategies they adopted (chapter 4). Nation-states and international governmental organizations favored assimilative reforms because of their structural connection to sovereignty. In contrast, nongovernmental organizations—less constrained or impressed by notions of sovereignty—initially tended toward coercive reform. Over time, as consensus developed that international intervention was appropriate, coercive strategies became less common throughout the global community.

The same theme of predictable variation in the effect of institutions is borne out in chapter 8. There I show that social context greatly influences the explanations women give for opposing FGC. For example, international organizations emphasize human rights as their basis for opposing FGC. Nevertheless, in areas where both Islam and FGC are institutionalized, women are more likely to articulate a medical explanation than a human rights explanation if they oppose the practice. Because a medical discourse is perceived as narrow and neutral, it is less threatening to local institutions than a human rights discourse. Once again, where one stands in relation to institutionalized principles determines whether and how those principles will be deployed.

Third, I argue that institutional conflict creates spaces for reform and resistance. This is important because critics argue that theories emphasizing institutions cannot explain change. In the case of FGC, change has occurred at the points where institutions contradict. I show how contradictions between institutionalized individualistic discourses and the institution of national autonomy led to "apolitical" medical intervention to reduce the incidence of FGC (chapter 3). This reframing of intervention technically preserved both individual rights and national sovereignty. Later, a similar result ensued when "individual rights" clashed with "family autonomy." In both cases, I argue that the individualistic discourse dominated and that both nation and family had to be reconceptualized to fit the new compromises.

I also consider the implications of these contradictions within different countries (Egypt, Tanzania, and the United States) (chapter 6). I show that relevance and resources have combined to fuel resistance to national reform when institutions disagree. Resistance is also important at the individual level (chapter 7). At the international and national level, contradictions arise between institutions within the same general Western meaning system (e.g., national autonomy, representative democracy, family autonomy, medicine, human rights). Resistance is much more powerful when these institutions contradict principles (Islam) or practices (FGC) institutionalized in *alternative* meaning systems. The most effective resistance to FGC reform efforts occurs in locations where alternative meaning systems are well developed and legitimated. I elaborate upon these three arguments below. I begin with a more detailed discussion of institutions.

Institutions

Many institutions figured prominently in debates over FGC: the nation-state and national autonomy, Western medicine, democracy, human rights, the family and family autonomy (privacy), Islam, and the practice of FGC itself. Institutions are social patterns or belief systems that accrete over human history, persist without active intervention, and are not eliminated when individuals fail to comply or agree with them. The origins of institutions are often unclear or unknown because institutions are age-old practices and beliefs. Their correctness is taken for granted. In fact, people remain true to institutions without any conscious reflection. For example, Americans get dressed every morning, drive on the right side of the road, and shake hands when they meet people. These actions are habitual—individuals do not consciously reflect on *whether* to do any of them; they simply do them. In terms of beliefs, institutions include both concepts (e.g., the United States) and values (e.g., human rights, democracy). Thousands of years of history—particularly Western history—lay the foundation for the assumptions and actions currently institutionalized in the international system.

Violating an institutionalized principle is likely to generate shock and anger among community members. Consequently, the ability of any individual to affect the institutionalized practices and beliefs in a profound way is slight. The failure to conform to an institution is seen as a defect in the actor, not the institution. Individuals may reflect on and disagree with institutions, but the institutions persist. For example, individuals may disagree with the assumptions of capitalism, but capitalism continues unabated. A more trivial example would be a woman in the United States who dislikes shaking hands because she fears the spread of germs. Her refusal to shake hands would raise eyebrows and cause her to be labeled "odd." It would not undermine the institutionalized practice of shaking hands. Institutions persist without active reflection by individuals and often despite active resistance by some individuals.

At one level, FGC is (or was until recently) institutionalized. Over time, the practice became so culturally embedded in some areas that individuals today cannot remember how it originated. It persists because these individuals take the practice for granted and do not actively reflect on whether to do it. If some individuals reject FGC (such as American and European ethnographers), the community is shocked and disgusted by those individuals. Their deviation from the institutionalized practice reflects poorly on them, not on the practice. Thus, the practice has all the components of an institution: it originated historically, its value is assumed, and individual deviations from it say more about the deviants than about the practice itself.

At the same time, at the international level other institutionalized ideas directly contradict the practice of FGC. Within international organizations, the idea that individuals are efficacious actors is taken for granted. Individuals are assumed to be self-directed, autonomous, and (incidentally) sexually capable and interested. Because these characteristics of individuals are so fundamental to the healthy functioning of society, they need special protection; hence the notion of human rights is critically important in the system. Further, it is assumed that individuals will value and guard their autonomy and inviolability, and that they will develop and express their sexual energies and passions fully and responsibly. When individuals fail to do this, it is evidence of their defectiveness or false consciousness, *not* evidence that these fundamental assumptions are incorrect. Because of the presumed universality of these individual characteristics, differences across cultures are considered shocking and defined as problematic.

The assumptions of universalism and rationality embedded in modern Western thought fuel these misunderstandings. As many others have noted, the institutions embedded in the international system stem from the culture of the Catholic Church, which itself carried on the traditions of the Roman Empire. Other universal religious traditions could have generated a different institutionalized system under favorable circumstances, but Western traditions, diffused through colonialism and other forms of hegemony, ended up playing this role. Over time, the rise of the state destroyed the organizational authority of the Church but absorbed and became dependent on a secularized version of the Church's principles. Now existing apart from a higher spiritual being, these universal secular principles nevertheless continue to define what ought to be, what is possible, and even what *is*.

The argument, then, is that historically derived institutionalized systems frame the collective mobilization of individuals. Unfortunately, most social scientists begin their analyses taking the Western assumptions for granted rather than critically reflecting on them. They assume that various sets of individuals have different mobilizing "interests." Successful mobilization is the result of a complex interaction of many factors, including resources, political opportunity, and status. Moral entrepreneurs are those individuals who are particularly effective at getting the world to notice "their" problems. History plays no part in these processes—rather, it seems as if individuals have the power to recreate the world from scratch every day. Further, failing to act in accordance with one's interests is considered problematic and puzzling.

On the other hand, even those who take institutions seriously have run into problems. These theorists tend to privilege the Western-oriented institutions embedded in the international system. Typically, they study only the effects of these international institutions and not the process through which those institutions come to influence recalcitrant nation-states and local communities. They rarely recognize the importance of local institutions such as FGC. The assumption is that "aberrant" institutions like FGC will inevitably disappear and therefore do not deserve much attention. Even if that were true—and I am not sure that it is—regard for local institutionalized practices is critically important in understanding globalization.[14] National policies will have little meaning in countries where their underlying spirit cannot be enacted. Giving women the right to vote is meaningless in a country where women are unable to move about freely. More to the point of this text, national laws banning FGC may be useless in countries if nearly all families in these countries continue to excise the genitals of their female children. Although it is true that in the long run reforms do tend to influence individuals, understanding why, when, and how this happens is essential. It provides insight into why and how Western ideologies are constantly expanding and where the limits to this expansion might be.

Institutions and National Policymaking

Institutions provide the starting point for this work's three theoretical contributions. Principles institutionalized in the international system are as important in shaping policy as the local political landscape of any particular country. (Local political landscapes are constituted by largely the same institutions as the result of centuries of institutional diffusion, but as I demonstrate here, some uniqueness persists and matters.) To understand why international institutions are so important for national policymaking, it is useful to think broadly about nation-states. Most local populations did not create a territorially bounded state from the ground up. Rather, early international actors (such as the Roman Empire, the Catholic Church, and colonial authorities) shaped the contours of current nation-states, especially outside of Europe. Even in places where there is a historical nexus between the local population and the modern state, that relationship often developed through the conversion of a formerly autocratic authority (e.g., monarchy, empire) into a representative government. The consequence is that there are no "natural," preexisting polities associated with most governments in the world. Historically, nation-states are just as likely to have been constructed by external forces as at the behest of local groups. The imagined link between local populations and local governments is based on a romanticized view of national histories. There may be much less connection than is commonly assumed.

Today, the extranational focus of nation-states is perpetuated by international organizations (Boli 1999). These organizations bolster a sense of community and commonality among nation-states. They define appropriate action for nation-states, based on the assumption that nation-states have similar concerns that can be worked out collectively. They operate on a logic of international equality, at least formally. For example, every nation-state, no matter how small or how poor, gets one vote in the U.N. General Assembly. States are allowed into the international "club" not on the basis of their links to local interests but rather because they are associated with a piece of territory that at some point was deemed a nation. When the United Nations accepts national representatives based on existing national borders, for example, in Africa, it perpetuates Africa's current geographic layout (see Rosberg and Jackson 1982). In essence, representation of people within particular territorial boundaries is assumed; except in egregious cases, it need not be demonstrated as a condition of acceptance.

Belonging to this global community has important implications for what nation-states say and do. Nations, and presumably people, take actions because those actions are, or at least could be interpreted as, "good" or "legitimate." In other words, actors are not driven solely by selfish interests; sometimes they are motivated by a historically derived sense of what is right. This is certainly true in the case of FGC; interest-based accounts have a hard time explaining why Western individuals would be interested in the practice at all. From a neo-institutionalist perspective, nation-states—like individuals—are socialized by the international community to value certain ends, take certain actions, and refrain from taking others (Finnemore 1996; Risse and Sikkink 1999).

This explains why the Egyptian state was willing to adopt a law against FGC despite considerable local opposition. Egypt—as a representative of the nation-state system—is an important carrier of the historically embedded principled ideas of that system. It is therefore not surprising that state actors in Egypt condemn the practice of FGC.

The Egyptian case also demonstrates that national policymaking is not *simply* a reaction to international pressure. International, national, and local cultures are inextricably intertwined. For example, for decades the international system presented no opposition to FGC. At the same time, opposition to FGC within Egypt dates back to at least the 1920s. In the recent period, the local Egyptian Organization for Human Rights and several Egyptian feminist organizations have been central in criticizing the practice. It would be greatly inaccurate to characterize all local Egyptians as supportive of FGC and all international actors as opposed to the practice. Even among those who agree that FGC should be eradicated, the explanations for that position vary dramatically. Not all opponents of FGC are "progressive"; not all advocates are "traditional." Further, "global" and "local" cultures are highly interpenetrated and mutually constitutive.[15]

Not surprisingly, then, national policymaking arises out of a complex interplay between "local" and "international" considerations. Although Egypt, like many other countries, did adopt an anti-FGC policy, its policymaking process looked quite different from those of other countries. Furthermore, the meaning of the policy, and reactions to it, took on unique qualities because of Egypt's national context. Egypt reacted to international pressure, but in a manner that distinguished it from other nation-states. An integrated theoretical perspective is necessary to fully explain global institutions, the interpenetration of global/local cultures, and the international/national impetus for national policymaking.

FGC is hardly an isolated example that supports the argument that local politics are driven by international concerns. There are many other examples. Strong military powers voluntarily limit their ability to use chemical weapons (Price 1997). Nations eager to spur more industrialization nevertheless voluntarily adopt stringent environmental laws (Frank, Schofer, and Hironaka 2000). Countries that derive substantial profits from the international drug trade subscribe to the war on drugs, even to the point of spraying harmful defoliants on much of their land. Often, a nation-state's authority is at least partly dependent on the legitimating power derived from linking into institutionalized beliefs. However, nations also tend to adopt policies consistent with global institutions because they are immersed within and constituted by those very institutions (Ramirez and McEneaney 1997; Frank and McEneaney 1999). In this context, the appropriateness of such actions is taken for granted. Global institutions determine what matters.

Structure and Perspective in Institutional Analysis

As noted above, this work also seeks to theorize how roles and structure influence the meaning and use of institutions. People around the globe see things very differently, even things as fundamental as what it means to be an individual. Agency is not something that can be taken for granted; it is a social construction linked uniquely to modernity and the West (Boyle and Meyer 1998; Meyer and Jepperson 2000). For example, the characters in Homer's *Iliad* did not see themselves as unique, self-motivated individuals but as internally fragmented beings whose actions were determined by gods (Friedland and Alford 1991). As this suggests, individuals were not always perceived as the fundamental building blocks of society, even in the West. In some societies today there is no conception of an abstract individual who exists and has value apart from particular social contexts.

To understand institutions and institutionalization, it is necessary to study areas of the world where individuality and individualism are not assumed. Because they construct individuals in ways that contrast with modern notions, these regions can provide the basis for a critical analysis of modernity. They also provide an important locus for testing neoinstitutionalism's premise that the conception of individuals is constantly expanding to include more actors and claims. Focusing on these areas of the world facilitates an understanding of the nature of "resistance" to modernizing trends.

A straightforward look at global changes over the course of the last century suggests that global institutions have enveloped individuals as well as nations. Individuals tend to embrace the same issues as those that concern international organizations: human rights, the environment, and so forth. Individuals who oppose mobilization around these issues are viewed as corrupt or ignorant by the rest of the world.

Nevertheless, one would expect more idiosyncrasy and resistance to institutionalized ideas among individuals than among nations. Global institutions are linked to the West and notions of modernity. They exalt individualism and the international structure of autonomous nation-states. Because nations are themselves part of the modern project, it makes sense that they would take the global institutions for granted. The same is unlikely to be true among individuals whose historical cultural milieu contrasts with or even opposes the principles of Western modernity. The case of FGC provides an opportunity to trace the meaning of the expansion of the global system for all individuals.

The Importance of Institutionalized Contradictions

Studying FGC also provides empirical insight into another aspect of the global system: the interrelationship between institutionalized principles. Global institutions are historically derived social constructions, and although perceived as universal, institutions often contradict each other. For example, in the case of FGC, although the institutionalized notion of individualism emphasizes human rights and calls for international organizations to intervene in national politics, the institutionalized system of sovereignty advises the opposite. Furthermore, if human rights is an institution internationally, certainly FGC itself is an institution locally in some parts of the world. Exploring the nature of these institutions and their interaction promises greater theoretical leverage to explain globalization processes.

One key principle—the idea of sovereign autonomy, i.e., local rule without outside interference—deserves special attention. This principle is ubiquitous but unique. It has become *the* legitimate basis for a counterargument to any international reform. Nations cannot argue that they favor FGC—any more than they can argue that they favor pollution, slavery, or torture.[16] However, nations can and do argue that FGC and these other issues do not warrant international intervention. Consequently, the idea of sovereign autonomy appears again and again in international debates. Whether and how the principle of sovereign autonomy affects international mobilization are key questions in any study of global cultural conflict.

The significance of sovereign autonomy is clear from its continued importance in organizing international intervention against FGC. Although it "lost" to the principle of universal human rights in the battle over FGC—international organizations did intervene to eradicate the practice—the principle of national autonomy still carried significant weight. It figured prominently in the strategies employed by international actors to bring nation-states into conformity with the anti-FGC norm. Certain types of international organizations were more influenced by the ideal of sovereign autonomy than others because of their structural linkage to the system of sovereign nation-states.

Contradictions inevitably arise in the everyday instantiations of substantive principles. Often, procedural principles define how those contradictions ought to be resolved. The contradictions between principles take on unique contours at different levels of analysis. At the international and national levels, the debate over FGC has been primarily procedural—whose moral vision would govern local actors? At the international level, national sovereignty and the somewhat related principle of cultural autonomy have sometimes been invoked to allow local governments to regulate local practices. Even when these institutionalized precepts were followed in the case of FGC, they merely allowed states to take unique positions on FGC; the principle did not privilege the *substance* of the varied positions. The ideal of sovereign autonomy protected unique local attributes not because they were substantively correct but because local authorities had jurisdiction. The sovereign autonomy ideal did not encourage debate or compromise among conflicting value systems. Even when commitment to sovereign autonomy was at its peak, the international community condemned FGC; it merely refused to act on that conviction. The key international question was procedural—whether the international community should be involved.

There was never any debate over the costs and benefits of the practice in the international system or any serious attempt to reach a compromise between contrasting cultures. The very idea of compromise was repugnant to most activists. Some Westerners might take this inability to compromise for granted, seeing no basis on which a compromise could occur. This is a mistake. In fact, compromise *is* possible and occurs frequently at the national and individual levels.

For example, rather than abandoning the practice altogether, many individuals are adopting milder forms of FGC in Sudan (Gruenbaum 2001, 182–83). Some individuals advocate banning the practice for children but making it legal for adults (Atoki 1995). Many alternatives to complete eradication exist. These have not been endorsed by international actors but may be important nationally and locally.

Another institutionalized conflict mirrored the conflict between sovereign autonomy and universal human rights. Representative democracy is also an institutionalized procedure. The actual laws produced by representative democracy are markedly less important than the process itself. In the case of FGC, this once again created a conflict because the democratic systems in some countries were not leading to a ban on FGC. For example, in Egypt, the parliament was unwilling to pass an anti-FGC law. Once again, a procedural principle failed to promote a substantive principle. The ideal of representative democracy was standing in the way of universal human rights. Ultimately, in both cases, the substantive institutionalized principle proved more powerful. International organizations decided to intervene locally to eradicate the practice, and national governments adopted anti-FGC policies with or without support from parliaments and legislatures.

At the national level, cultural conflict has fueled the decoupling of state policy from action and caused seemingly similar policies to have very different meanings, depending on the countries adopting them. The brief history of Egypt's actions illustrates how states came to view their roles in eradication efforts very differently over time. In 1990, the Egyptian government expressed opposition to FGC but claimed the practice was not its responsibility. By 1996, the Egyptian government was an active player in eradication efforts. This change in the government's position resulted from the complex interplay between all forms of international actors: international governmental organizations; nongovernmental organizations, including the media and religious organizations; and states. At the national level, sovereign autonomy acquires more substance and becomes a concrete basis for decoupling policy from action. The conflict between rights and culture directly influences the effectiveness of national policies.

At the individual level, the unique national attributes privileged but not explored in international arenas have their greatest impact. These attributes provide a specific alternative meaning system to the one carried by the international system (for example, Islam in some communities). Although the influence of these alternative meaning systems at the international level is merely procedural, at the individual level there is no such limitation; for at least some Muslim communities, the effect at this level is substantive. Cultural conflict manifests itself as powerful alternative meaning systems at the individual level, with profound implications for how individuals view FGC as well as themselves. Using Demographic and Health Survey data, I demonstrate that religious background has an important impact on attitudes toward FGC and whether women circumcise their daughters. Even more important, in some African countries, being Islamic mediates the effects of other variables, such as exposure to institutions based on Western principles. This is true despite the agreement among most Islamic clerics that Islam does not condone FGC (Bashir 1996).

Institutional contradictions can provide the basis for massive shifts in values and beliefs (Friedland and Alford 1991). How does this happen? When activists can demonstrate inconsistencies in the application of principled ideas—which is possible when the ideas contradict —they have more leverage to push for reform. Since World War II, the international debate over FGC has centered on the authority of nations, science, and individuals. Although initially FGC was a matter of sovereign autonomy, Western feminists were able to exploit the contradiction between the idea of autonomy and the idea of individual human rights to create a "space" for anti-FGC mobilization. Over time, as the links between FGC and human rights were clarified, the balance in ideals shifted to favor individual human rights and international intervention.

The issue of FGC has been highly contested because it touches on many different issues: the sacredness of the family; women's rights as human rights; state obligations in the "private" sphere; human sexuality; gender inequality; race; the arrogance of the West toward other cultures; the West's view of people in other cultures as "exotic others"; postmodern colonialism; and cultural autonomy (see Gunning 1990–91; Silbey 1997). Precisely because of this intense conflict, FGC can provide unique insights into the operation of global-local connections in the international system.

This book is not so much about FGC as about the international, national, and individual responses to the practice. The book is organized by levels of analysis, beginning with the "macro" international level, moving next to the national level, and concluding at the "micro" individual level of analysis. Chapter 2 provides background information on the practice of FGC. It explains the variety of physical procedures that come under that heading. It traces the history of the practices and looks at the social contexts in which they occur today. Chapter 2 also describes the medical implications of the different forms of FGC and compares them with male circumcision. Finally, the chapter describes early eradication efforts.

Chapters 3 through 8 explain the unique development and impact of the debate over FGC at each of three levels of analysis—the international, national, and individual levels.

Chapters 3 and 4 focus primarily on the international level. They pick up on the historical development of opposition to FGC, addressing the question of what made a radical change in perspective possible. As time passed, the relative weight of institutionalized principles shifted so that concern for individuals took precedence, first over national autonomy and later over the inviolability of the family. This historical trajectory is interesting because discourses that were rejected out of hand during early time periods later became dominant. This also hints at a pattern that may be common across a number of issues: new obligations may simultaneously undermine the autonomy of collectivities while increasing their durability. Chapter 3, in a theme echoed throughout the book, concludes that global institutions such as national sovereignty do not disappear but that the relationship between institutions can change dramatically over specified time periods.

Chapter 4 demonstrates how certain types of international organizations were more influenced by the idea of sovereign autonomy than others (Boyle and Preves 2000; Boyle and Liu 2002). Organizations' varying linkages to the system of sovereign nation-states influenced their choice of mobilizing strategies. Specifically, the greater its dependence on the sovereignty system, the more weight an actor assigned to sovereign autonomy. The chapter also illustrates the procedural character of the debate at this level; the idea of sovereign autonomy protected unique local attributes but provided no support for those local attributes to be substantively persuasive in discussions of global values.

Linking international mobilization with national policymaking, chapter 5 explores the diffusion of anti-FGC policies during the 1990s. Recent international activism attacking FGC has been very successful in getting countries to adopt policies against FGC. A few key countries adopted these policies in the 1980s and then, over the course of a decade, other countries in the world followed suit. International organizations played an important role in reaching this result.

Moving to the national level, chapter 6 focuses particularly on the cases of Egypt, Tanzania, and the United States to illustrate the national policy extension of the international debate over FGC (Boyle, Songora, and Foss 2001). At this level, culture becomes a key factor in the decoupling of policy and action in countries where anti-FGC policies are most relevant. For example, after CNN internationally broadcast the 10-year-old girl's circumcision in Cairo, President Mubarak found himself in the uncomfortable position of proposing anti-FGC legislation to an unsympathetic Egyptian parliament. When the legislation failed, Mubarak's health minister adopted a decree limiting the practice. Although the decree was a compromise between local interests and international pressure, allowing FGC in limited circumstances, it was very controversial both locally and internationally. Its enforcement will be contested.

My argument is that functionality of a proposed policy and national standing in the international system combine to influence the level of contestation generated by reform efforts. Specifically, I argue that, all else being equal, policies will be more contested when the reform serves a concrete function locally—that is, when it is relevant to local individuals. Further, among countries where a policy has local relevance, a nation's standing in the international system will also be critically important. I theorize that conflict over new policies will be greater in countries with more leverage in the international system. These nations have more ability to actually shape rather than simply receive policy edicts. In addition, individuals in these nations are likely to have more resources on average, which provides more ability to mobilize opposition to international norms. At the national level, sovereign autonomy acquired more substance and became a concrete basis for decoupling policy from action. The conflict between rights and culture directly influenced the effectiveness of national policies.

Chapters 7 and 8 explore the individual level, where the unique national attributes privileged but not explored in international arenas have their greatest impact (Boyle, McMorris, and Gómez 2002; Boyle, Hoeschen, and Carbone 2002). These attributes, sometimes including a commitment to Islam, provide a specific alternative meaning system to the one carried by the international system. Using case studies from the literature and Demographic and Health Survey data, I demonstrate that religious and cultural backgrounds have an important impact on attitudes toward FGC and whether women circumcise their daughters. Even more important, these factors mediate the effects of other variables, such as exposure to Western principles.

Ultimately, the central focus of this book is exploring, at different levels of analysis, the varied meaning of anti-FGC policies. The evidence is both qualitative and quantitative, including an analysis of existing academic articles and books, the activist literature, reports of international organizations, and interviews. It also includes a comprehensive data set of more than one thousand articles on FGC from international newspapers. For evidence at the individual level of analysis, Demographic and Health Survey data from six African countries and detailed case studies from the existing literature provide information on individual attitudes and behavior.

FGC became a celebrated cause internationally despite early hesitance to act and pockets of opposition to eradication efforts. The practice has existed for more than two thousand years, and 130 million women alive today have experienced it. Nevertheless, in a short span of decades, FGC has become a source of embarrassment in the nation-state system, and those nation-states whose citizens engage in FGC have gone to considerable lengths to demonstrate their disdain for it. The transformation of approaches to FGC is thus a critical example of profound social change occurring in the context of globalization. It provides an important starting point for linking theoretical ideas across international, national, and individual spheres of reality.

TWO

Understanding Female Genital Cutting

I think I am safe in saying that none of us who has studied the practice in its context are so theoretically myopic or inhumane as to advocate its continuance . . . Understanding the practice is not the same as condoning it. It is, I believe, as crucial to effecting the operation's eventual demise that we understand the context in which it occurs as much as its medical sequelae.

—Janice Boddy, "Body Politics," 1991

Although the precise origins of FGC are unclear, the practice dates back to antiquity (Lightfoot-Klein 1989). FGC is deeply embedded in the culture of a number of central African nations. FGC is practiced widely in twenty-five countries and by a majority of families in fourteen countries (U.S. Department of State 1999). Although the practice is currently prevalent primarily in African and Asian countries, FGC was performed on white women in Western nations as recently as the 1950s, as a medical treatment for nymphomania and depression (Barker-Benfield 1976, 1975). In the modern era, the practice continues to occur in the West in small numbers, predominantly among certain groups of new immigrants. The World Health Organization estimates that worldwide more than 130 million women and girls living today have undergone some form of genital cutting (World Health Organization 1997).

Controversy rages over what to call the practice. Communities that engage in FGC use different terms (Gruenbaum 2001, 2–4). The Arabic words most commonly used to describe the practice are *tahur,* or the variant *tahara,* which translates as "purification." These terms suggest the achievement of cleanliness through ritual. In a number of communities, FGC is referred to as *sunna.* This means "tradition," spe-

cifically a tradition that the Prophet Mohammed engaged in or supported during his lifetime. The practice has many other names derived from an array of different languages.

Often, a community uses the same or related terms for FGC and
male circumcision. As a consequence, Westerners initially referred to
the practice as "female circumcision." Activists object to this phrase
because it exaggerates the similarities between the male and female
operations. FGC typically reduces or eliminates sexual sensation for
women. Male circumcision does not have the same effect. To distinguish FGC from male circumcision and to highlight its ill effects,
Fran Hosken, founder of the Women's International Network, coined
the term "female genital mutilation." This term is still widely used
by actors in the international system, for example, the World Health
Organization. Nevertheless, African feminists and scholars have criticized "female genital mutilation" for being ethnocentric, and many
activists and scholars now avoid the term. For example, Obiora (1997)
and Gruenbaum (2001) continue to use the term "female circumcision" in deference to African cultures. Gunning (1990–91) refers to
the practices as "female genital surgeries" to emphasize the similarity
to unnecessary cosmetic surgeries in the West. Others adopt the term
"female genital modifications" because the acronym "FGM" has become widely recognized.

I choose to use the term "female genital cutting" because Asma
Abdel Halim[1] at the U.S. Agency for International Development specifically requested that I use that term and because it is an accurate,
nonpoliticized description of the practice (see Bibbings 1995). I use
"circumcise" as a verb because it is widely understood, but I acknowledge its inaccuracy. I should also note that when I mention the "practice" or "procedure" of FGC, I am actually referring to an entire range
of different practices and procedures.

In fact, there are many types of FGC. At one time, these were
grouped into two categories, *sunna* and Pharaonic, but today it is common to distinguish three categories (Toubia and Izett 1998). Across
the three categories, *sunna* is the least invasive procedure and is most
comparable to male circumcision. In *sunna* cuttings, the prepuce, or
hood, of the clitoris is removed. This type of cutting is common
among the Bedouin in Israel (Asali et al. 1995). It was also the type

of cutting performed in the nineteenth century in the United States (Barker-Benfield 1975). Nahid Toubia has suggested that this form of FGC is rare in Africa. There is some confusion about the term because in many communities local individuals use *sunna* to describe FGC that is generally more serious than what writers refer to as *sunna* cuttings in the academic literature.

The second type of FGC is "genital excision" or "clitoridectomy." This category involves the removal of some or all of the clitoris and the labia minora, leaving the labia majora intact. Clitoridectomies vary in their degree of seriousness. This is the most common form of FGC in Africa.

"Infibulation," or "Pharaonic," cuttings are the most extreme form of FGC. These cuttings involve the excision of the clitoris, labia minora, and labia majora, followed by the sewing together of the raw edges of the vulva, leaving only a small hole through which urine and menstrual fluid may pass. Infibulation is common in the horn of Africa region (Somalia, Sudan, Ethiopia, Eritrea, and Djibouti). Only 15–20 percent of circumcised women are infibulated. If done "properly," infibulation makes sexual intercourse impossible. Women who are infibulated must be deinfibulated at the time of their marriage. Common complications from FGC include shock, bleeding, infection, and—for infibulation—delayed problems such as menstrual pain, urinary tract infections, painful intercourse, and difficulties in childbirth. On rare occasions, complications arising from FGC can even result in death.

Fundamentally, FGC is, or at least has been, normative in most of the areas where it occurs. Many stories relate the shock and revulsion that greets female scholars from the West in these regions when their lack of circumcision is discovered. A Westerner in northern Sudan who was invited to attend a circumcision related the following response to her lack of enthusiasm: "Bakhritta, sensing that my interpretation of events was not hers, could not believe it. 'Don't you believe it's a good thing to do, Melissa?' And she said this with amazement rather than aggression. Similarly, Khadiga said, 'Don't you think it's fine and lovely?' genuinely surprised that there could be any other interpretation" (Parker 1995, 510). The surprise of the women in this example is well matched by the shock and revulsion of Americans when they first learn of the practice. The following outraged letter to the editor of the *Sacramento Bee* regarding whether FGC should be a basis for asylum in the United States provides one example: "Re: 'Mutilation weighed as grounds for asylum' . . . Weighed? Weighed? What is there to weigh? There cannot be any degree of pro or con with this issue of female genital mutilation, only an emphatic no to this barbaric, sexist, misogynist practice."[2] The shock that occurs when individuals from different cultures learn about FGC or the lack thereof is a dramatic illustration of culture in conflict.[3]

The History of Female Genital Cutting

FGC can be traced back as far as the second century B.C., when a geographer, Agatharchides of Cnidus, wrote about FGC as it occurred among tribes residing on the western coast of the Red Sea (modern-day Egypt) (Mackie 1996). Based on the current geographic locations of FGC, the practice appears to have originated there with infibulation and spread southward and westward while diminishing to clitoridectomy (Mackie 1996). (In the modern period, Egyptians practice clitoridectomies rather than infibulation.)

Some surmise that FGC is rooted in the Pharaonic belief in the bisexuality of the gods (Meinardus 1967; Assaad 1980). According to this belief, mortals reflected this trait of the gods—every individual possessed both a male and a female soul. The feminine soul of the man was located in the prepuce of the penis; the male soul of the woman was located in the clitoris. For healthy gender development, the female soul had to be excised from the man and the male soul excised from the woman. Circumcision was thus essential for boys to become men; and girls, women (Meinardus 1967, 388–89).

Another theory is that FGC originated as a way to control women's sexuality. Infibulation was thought to control women's desire for sex and thus prevent premarital sex and keep women faithful to their husbands after marriage (Kijo-Bisimba, Lee, and Wallace 1999; Dorkenoo 1995; El Dareer 1982). To the extent that FGC made men masters over female sexual function, it historically reinforced the idea that wives are their husbands' private property (Lightfoot-Klein 1989). This belief predates Islam, which specifically rejects such a characterization of women (Bielefeldt 1995).

In the pattern of its adoption, there is a clear connection between FGC and slavery (Mackie 1996). Prior to the rise of Islam, Egyptians raided territories to the south for slaves, and Sudanic slaves were exported to areas along the Persian Gulf. Eventually, an Islamic slave trade developed in the same area, delivering concubines and servants from the Sudanic region to Egypt and Arabia. Reports from the fifteenth and sixteenth centuries suggest that female slaves sold for a higher price if they were "sewn up" in a way that made them unable to conceive (Mackie 1996). Modesty conventions like FGC, although predating Islam, corresponded with Islamic ideals of family honor and female chastity and seclusion (Assaad 1980). This may have contributed to the widespread adoption of the practice in some areas.

Further, the Egyptian elite had a proclivity for populating large harems with infibulated slaves. Initially, the women in the harems were local women. After the region converted to Islam, however, this was no longer possible because Islam prohibits Muslims from enslaving other Muslims. Thus, as Islam spread, slave traders were forced to reach farther into the African continent to find non-Muslim slaves to populate the harems. Presumably, the slave traders introduced FGC to these more remote populations to enhance the value of the women as slaves. Both Islamic conversion and FGC spread along these expanding slave routes (Mackie 1996; Hicks 1993).

But why does the practice continue hundreds of years after the disappearance of the slave trade that fueled it? The most encompassing explanation is that the practice continues because it is a tradition (Bibbings 1995, 155; Carr 1997, 27). Although few individuals who practice FGC are aware of the early mythology of bisexuality, they do stereotype uncircumcised girls as more masculine (Assaad 1980, 4). Further, FGC accentuates the differences between men and women, and generally only women are allowed to be present during circumcisions. In some communities, men are harshly punished (even executed) for witnessing FGC.[4] Where FGC is practiced, it is nearly always seen as part of a woman's preparation for marriage. Seventy-four percent of married women in a recent Egyptian survey believed that husbands preferred "circumcised" women (Carr 1997), and similar findings appear in Tanzania (Kijo-Bisimba, Lee, and Wallace 1999). As this suggests, men play an important indirect role in the perpetuation of the practice by insisting that their wives be circumcised (A'Haleem 1992).[5] This is true despite the fact that mothers typically take responsibility for having their daughters circumcised. Other factors that perpetuate the practice include the ceremonies surrounding the practice; FGC may be one of the few times when a woman (or girl) is the center of attention in her community (Mabala and Kamazima 1995). Some sort of celebration, ranging from a sedate women's tea party to a gala for the entire community, nearly always precedes or follows FGC. Until recently, the practice was so taken for granted that in many areas *not* circumcising one's daughters would have been considered poor parenting.

In addition, in nearly every location, FGC is an income-generating activity for some. The individuals who earn money from the practice have an incentive to perpetuate it. On one occasion in Tanzania, 73 circumcisors surrendered all their equipment to the Same district commissioner after being promised by the Network against Female Genital Mutilation that they would be given loans to start other businesses. Ultimately, the promise was not fulfilled, and they have threatened to go back to performing the practice.[6]

Beyond these common elements, the current manifestation of FGC differs across locations. The practice is constructed in at least two very distinct ways, with some communities practicing what seems to be a combination of the two types. This first type is linked to Islam. Islam is an encompassing moral code that emphasizes women's modesty and chastity. Virginity is considered the most precious possession of an unmarried woman, and FGC is believed to protect that virginity (Assaad 1980). These communities are often characterized by a segregation of the sexes, and FGC tends to be a private affair. Girls are not circumcised in groups but rather individually. Male circumcision in these communities is also a private event, so there is no "cohort" of boys being circumcised at the same time a particular girl is undergoing FGC. Male circumcision tends to generate more celebration than FGC. Cleanliness and purity are seen as positive attributes of FGC. FGC is also believed to increase male sexual pleasure. Although FGC did not originate with Islam, its continuation is tied up with Islamic beliefs in some areas (Boyle, McMorris, and Gómez 2002; Coleman 1999).

In these locations, such as northern Sudan, girls are circumcised at a young age, typically between five and ten years old. Another example of this type of community occurs in Egypt, where a recent survey found that 72 percent of married women believe that FGC is a religious tradition (Carr 1997). The type of FGC is typically infibulation or clitoridectomy. Boddy (1982) argues that "virginity" has a somewhat different meaning in northern Sudan than in the United States. Virginity is more about being sexually inaccessible than about never having had sex. Thus, when women are reinfibulated after giving birth, their virginity—inaccessibility—is restored. Historically, FGC might be justified in these areas as protecting a woman from her natural "oversexed nature," but recent Demographic and Health Survey data from Egypt suggest that this explanation may no longer be particularly prevalent (see Assaad 1980; Carr 1997).

FGC manifests itself somewhat differently in other communities. These communities, which are rarely Islamic, see FGC as a rite of passage into adulthood (see, e.g., Robertson 1996; Walley 1997). Girls might be circumcised when they reach puberty or right before they are married. Thus, they tend to be older, fourteen to sixteen years of age, than girls in the communities just mentioned. The form of FGC is nearly always clitoridectomy. In some of these areas, individuals believe that people are born with two souls—an adult soul and a child soul. FGC and male circumcision are believed to remove the child soul and thereby facilitate maturation. In some places, such as parts of Sierra Leone, the circumcision is part of the initiation into a secret society (Ahmadu 2000). Consequently, there is often an education program accompanying FGC that instructs the "initiates" in the ways of womanhood.

It is also typical in these communities for girls to be circumcised in age cohorts. Although girls and boys are segregated, their ceremonies often happen at the same time and are preceded or followed by a community-wide celebration. Thus, FGC and male circumcision solidify relationships between members of particular age cohorts. Another important distinction is that, in some of these areas, virginity is not a major concern. For example, among the Sabaot of Kenya, sexual petting leading to orgasm is allowed prior to marriage (although penetration is forbidden). It would not be uncommon for a woman to have some sexual experience before she is circumcised. The point of FGC in these areas seems to be creating solidarity and, in some cases, leaving behind the pleasures of childhood to prepare for the responsibilities of adulthood.

Some sources are documenting yet a third social context for FGC, one less common than the preceding two: girls seeking FGC because it is fashionable. Recently, in Myabé in southern Chad near the border of the Central African Republic, girls whose mothers are not circumcised have begun to seek the practice for themselves. Sometimes their actions actually go against the wishes of their parents. Leonard, who spent some time in the village, concludes that peer pressure is the basis for undergoing the practice there. As one of the village girls told her, "Girls who have done it won't let you dance with them" (2000, 216). The desire to not be a social outcast spurs girls to seek FGC for themselves.

These differences in the meaning of FGC may affect the nature of resistance to international reform efforts. They should also influence eradication strategies. Given the varied meanings assigned to the practice in different locations, it makes sense that strategies effective in one area may not be effective in all areas.

Religion

Whether Islam requires FGC is a contested question (Boddy 1991). The practice predates Islam, does not occur in most Middle Eastern countries, and is not explicitly required by the Koran. Further, as just explained, in Africa groups other than Muslims practice FGC. Many Coptic Christian women in Egypt, for instance, have been circumcised (Assaad 1980). In Tanzania, where 20 of 120 ethnic groups practice FGC, regions that are predominantly *Christian* actually have the highest percentages of circumcised women. The only region in Tanzania in which a large percentage of Muslims coincides with a relatively high rate of FGC is Tanga, where 25.1 percent of the women are circumcised. Thus, there are many Muslims in Africa who do not practice FGC, and there are other religious groups (including Christians) that do engage in the practice.

Nevertheless, some Islamic leaders advocated the practice historically, and, for the historic reasons just outlined, its occurrence does coincide to some extent with the rise of Islam in Africa (see Assaad 1980; Coleman 1998; Boyle, McMorris, and Gómez 2002). Further, my colleagues and I recently analyzed Demographic and Health Survey data in five African countries and found that being Christian was a strong predictor of women rejecting FGC—in both attitudes and behavior (Boyle, McMorris, and Gómez 2002). Because of the controversy surrounding this discussion, it is worthwhile to consider the nature of Islam more closely.

Islamic law, known as *shari'a*, is based on two sources (Bielefeldt 1995). The primary source is the Koran, which contains God's own proclamations to the Prophet Mohammed. The Koran says nothing supportive of or in opposition to FGC. Muslims also turn for guidance to a collection of the sayings and practices of Mohammed called the *Sunna*. Each individual saying or custom is termed a *hadith*. Not all *hadith* are considered authentic. Muslim scholars spend a considerable amount of time researching the genealogy of various *hadith* to determine whether each is truly traceable to Mohammed (Coleman 1999). For a *hadith* to be considered authoritative, the genealogy must demonstrate an uninterrupted connection to the Prophet.

There is a *hadith* that addresses the practice of FGC.[7] It describes Mohammed suggesting to a female circumcisor that excision is "allowed" but should not be "overdone" because a more limited cutting "brings more radiance to the face . . . and is . . . better for the husband" (Abu-Sahlieh 1996, cited in Coleman 1998, 731, n. 41). The *hadith* also suggests that Mohammed called genital cutting a *makrumah*, or honorable deed for women. This *hadith* is contested, however, because the relevant authority is obscure and its genealogy questionable. Nevertheless, the *hadith* has had an important effect in parts of Africa. For example, a *fatwa* issued by an important Islamic cleric in Egypt in 1950 declared: "Female circumcision is an Islamic practice mentioned in the tradition of the Prophet, and sanctioned by Imams and Jurists, in spite of differences on whether it is a duty or a *sunna* [tradition]. We support the practice as *sunna* and sanction it in view

of its effect on attenuating the sexual desire in women and directing to the desirable moderation" (Assaad 1980, 5). As noted in chapter 1, Sheikh Gad el-Haqq, the head of Al-Azhar University in the mid-
1990s, issued a similar *fatwa*. Despite these periodic references to the
controversial *hadith*, most Islamic clerics refute the notion that Mohammed condoned FGC (Bashir 1996). Thus, Boddy's (1991) assessment that the practice is not Islamic but is *religious* for many of the
women who practice it is perhaps most accurate.

Medical Complications

A recent World Health Organization report related a number of short-
and long-term health consequences from FGC (Toubia and Izett
1998). The risk of these problems is reduced but not eliminated when
FGC is performed in modern medical facilities. Although serious
complications can accompany any form of FGC, infibulated women
are especially vulnerable. Further, when complications arise during or
after infibulation, they tend to be more serious and last longer than
complications arising from other forms of FGC. Having a trained professional conduct the procedures reduces but does not eliminate the
health risks.

Severe bleeding is the most common immediate complication of
FGC. One study estimated that hemorrhaging accounted for 25 percent of all complications. Because children tend to move during the
cutting, injuries to neighboring organs also sometimes occur. Urine
retention, lasting for hours or days, can occur but is usually reversible.
Infection is also very common, with the degree of infection varying
from a superficial wound infection to a generalized blood infection.
Using a sterilized instrument to perform FGC greatly decreases this
risk. Because the genitals are highly sensitive, the procedure is extremely painful when performed without anesthesia. Even when anesthesia is used, the application of anesthesia itself can be very painful
(Toubia and Izett 1998, 26–27).

Long-term complications arising from clitoridectomies include a
failure to heal, abscesses, cysts, and keloids (Toubia and Izett 1998,
27). Abscesses occur when an infection becomes buried under the
wound and usually require a surgical incision and proper dressing as

treatment. Cysts result from the embedding of skin tissue in the scar. The glands in the skin will continue to secrete body fluids under the scar and form a cyst or sac full of cheesy material. Keloids are the excessive growth of scar tissue. Although cysts and keloids are not serious health risks, as disfigurements they can be very distressing. A clitoridectomy may also result in urinary tract infections or a painful scar neuroma.

In addition to these complications, infibulation—the most serious form of FGC—carries other long-term health consequences. These include reproductive tract infections, painful menstruation, chronic urinary tract obstructions, and incontinence (Toubia and Izett 1998, 28–29). Infibulation also requires that a woman be deinfibulated prior to childbirth. If an experienced attendant is unavailable to deinfibulate, obstructed labor causing moderate to severe complications for mother and child can result.

Currently, there is no evidence that FGC is a major contributor to the spread of AIDS, hepatitis B, or other blood-borne diseases (Toubia and Izett 1998, 30–31). Although some have hypothesized that FGC (especially infibulation) may increase rates of maternal and neonatal mortality, there are currently no studies demonstrating this connection. Fundamentally, it is difficult to separate delivery complications that result from pregnancy among very young girls and those that result from FGC.

Implications for Sexuality

Contrary to the perception of some Westerners, FGC is not necessarily associated with a complete lack of sexual function (Obermeyer 1999). Lightfoot-Klein began her interviews with Sudanese women in the late 1970s with the assumption that circumcised women would not enjoy sex, but she soon realized that this preconception was incorrect. When she asked one woman in a preliminary interview whether she was able to enjoy sexual intercourse, the woman reacted with uncontrolled mirth. The reaction was contagious; soon Lightfoot-Klein, her translator, and the woman were all rolling on the floor laughing and hooting. When they managed to calm down, the translator explained, "She says you must be completely *mad* to ask her a question like that! She says: 'A *body is a body* and no circumcision can change that. No matter what they cut away from you—they cannot change that!'" (1989, 25–26, emphasis in original). The incident brought home to Lightfoot-Klein that she was dealing with real people with real lives and real relationships. Ultimately, close to 90 percent of the Sudanese women she interviewed claimed to have achieved orgasm at some time in their lives. Although she surmised that this number was too high, it does indicate that the effect of FGC on sexuality is much more complex than a simple anatomy lesson.

Other studies also suggest that FGC does not necessarily eliminate sexual pleasure. In Egypt, 94 percent of the 54 women interviewed by Assaad (1980) said that they enjoyed sex. Earlier surveys in Egypt had found that about 41 percent of the women surveyed had experienced orgasm (Obermeyer 1999). In a survey of the Ibo in Nigeria, 59 percent of circumcised women reported experiencing orgasm, compared with 69 percent of uncircumcised women. In all of these cases, the women had undergone some form of clitoridectomy.

As with other health consequences, with respect to sexuality, infibulation appears to be the most debilitating form of FGC. One study found that although more than 80 percent of women who were infibulated had never experienced orgasm, only 10 percent of women with mild clitoridectomies had never achieved orgasm (the same percentage as among uncircumcised women) (Shandall 1967). El Dareer (1982) found that among a sample of north Sudan infibulated women, 50 percent of the women reported no sexual pleasure and 23 percent were indifferent to sexual intercourse, but the remainder experienced pleasure from intercourse all or some of the time. More studies, especially studies involving comparisons across groups, are needed to precisely determine the varying effect of FGC on female sexuality.

One might wonder how it is physiologically possible for women to enjoy sex after FGC. One possibility is that some portion of the clitoris may still be intact after the procedure. For example, Gruenbaum (2001) found that some midwives in Sudan did not remove the entire clitoris beneath the infibulation when they performed FGC. They feared that the girl would hemorrhage if they removed the clitoris entirely. Another possibility is that the remaining erogenous zones of the body experience enhanced sensitivity to compensate for the lack of sensation in the altered clitoris. Certainly, a woman's relationship with her spouse plays an important role. Women who are happily married tend to report more enjoyment from sex, whether or not they are circumcised.

Psychological Consequences

As with sex, the psychological effects of FGC are largely undefined (Toubia and Izett 1998). The FGC event is often traumatic and can leave a lifelong emotional scar. For example, a twenty-one-year-old woman interviewed by Lightfoot-Klein reported that she thought circumcision was a crime. After her infibulation, she read books on sexuality and began to realize what she had lost: "Her feelings of rage are quite clear as she talks about this. She expresses hatred toward her parents for allowing this to be done to her" (1989, 249). Similar expressions of outrage and disappointment are common in autobiographies and ethnographic accounts.

At the same time, many women also have positive associations with the event, such as being the center of attention, bonding with peers, and receiving material gifts (Mabala and Kamazima 1995). Often, mothers try to diminish the trauma of the event for their children. As Parker, who witnessed several infibulations in Sudan, noted: "People clearly sympathized with the girl's pain—for they themselves had all been pharaonically circumcised—and everyone was gentle with her. In fact Ziyarra [her mother] never left her daughter for the two hours or so that I was there. *Mat guum, mat guum* 'Don't leave, don't leave,' the girl kept saying, hanging her arms around her mother's neck. And she held her tight, gently assuring her that she would not go" (Parker 1995, 509–10). Another example comes from an American teacher in Kikhome village in Kenya whose female and male students told her with "boisterous pride" of their circumcision ceremonies immediately upon her arrival. Many ethnographic accounts confirm that special memories often surround FGC.

At least until recently, there were also areas where the pressure to circumcise one's daughters was society-wide. In these areas, girls who were not circumcised could face psychological hardships; they could become social outcasts. In some ethnic groups, uncircumcised women are perceived as unclean and impure (Wada 1992). In others, for example the Masai in Tanzania, an uncircumcised woman is never called "mother," even if she has children. Among the Kuria of Tanzania, uncircumcised women are assigned a very degrading name and laughed at by other women when they go to bathe (Mabala and Kamazima 1995). In still other ethnic groups, such women are barred from funerals and other important traditional activities. As these examples indicate, FGC is an important measure of status within a number of different ethnic groups.

Relationship to Other Types of Genital Cutting

Anti-FGC activists have gone to great lengths to distinguish FGC from male circumcision. Primarily they argue that FGC does more harm than male circumcision, is not a religious requirement, and is done with the explicit purpose of oppressing women. For example, a 1997 report from the Demographic and Health Survey program stated that male circumcision is "less invasive" than FGC, which carries "more serious physical and psychological effects." The report continued by suggesting that analogous operations for men "would involve the partial or complete removal of the penis" rather than just the foreskin (Carr 1997, 2).

Nevertheless, there are some fundamental similarities between FGC and male circumcision. Both practices involve the removal of healthy tissue from a child's genitals, often without anesthesia. Both procedures are considered medically unnecessary. Some of the most frequent health complications are similar: infection, hemorrhaging, urine retention, and accidental damage to nearby organs. A recent *New York Times* article reported that the number of deaths related to botched *male* circumcisions is on the rise in South Africa (a country where FGC is not practiced).

Not all the similarities between FGC and male circumcision pertain to basic health concerns; some are related to beliefs and traditions. In Africa, boys and girls are often, but not always, circumcised at the same age as part of their initiation into adulthood. Both of the procedures are sometimes, but not always, motivated by religious beliefs. A desire for social conformity is often important in the decision to have either male or female children circumcised. Further, it is important to recognize that there are several different types of FGC. Although infibulation and some forms of clitoridectomy are comparable to male castration, *sunna* cuttings are in fact fairly physically comparable to male circumcision (Coleman 1999).

Despite their differences, then, it is perhaps not surprising that increasing attention to FGC has led to renewed discussions about other genital surgeries. Concerned about the negative health consequences of male circumcision among Muslim immigrants, Sweden recently passed a law mandating the medicalization of that practice. Only trained professionals are now authorized to conduct male circumcisions in Sweden, and they must administer an analgesic or an anesthetic. In the United States, a group of women unsuccessfully challenged the federal anti-FGC law on the grounds that it violated the equal protection clause of the U.S. Constitution. The agenda of these women was to use the statute to condemn male circumcision.

The U.S. legislation has also been used by groups of intersex individuals (i.e., hermaphrodites) to argue against binary sex surgeries (Preves 1999). These surgeries are designed to unambiguously assign hermaphroditic babies to a particular sex. Until very recently, when children were born with genitalia that were neither clearly male nor clearly female, it was routine to surgically alter the genitalia. The hermaphroditic condition, although socially awkward, is rarely life-threatening. As with FGC, the surgeries can permanently reduce sexual pleasure. Groups such as Hermaphrodites with Attitude are trying to demedicalize the intersex condition. They use the U.S. ban on FGC to support their position. These examples illustrate how the expansion of rights to prohibit one particular practice expands to incorporate many additional claims.

Early Eradication Efforts

Early responses to FGC stem from Western roots, with initial opposition instigated by Catholic missionaries in Egypt in the seventeenth century (Mackie 1996). These missionaries reportedly forbade FGC among converts because they believed it was a Jewish practice. When the church began to lose converts as a result of this policy, a special investigation by the Vatican resulted in the policy's reversal. The investigation purportedly determined that Egyptian women's oversized genitals justified excision (Mackie 1996). Although not linked to the same false conception of anatomy, the opposition of Christian missionaries in Kenya to FGC in the early nineteenth century also failed to eradicate the practice (Murray 1976; Natsoulas 1998). Missionaries of the Church of Scotland mobilized against the practice among the Kikuyu of Kenya in 1906 but merely politicized the issue rather than decreasing its occurrence (El Dareer 1982, 92).

Another attempt at eradication among Christian converts in Kenya occurred in the 1920s but met a similar fate (Keck and Sikkink 1998). Jomo Kenyatta, who later became Kenya's first president, took this opportunity to cast the practice in a favorable light. In his nationalist treatise, *Facing Mount Kenya: The Tribal Life of the Gikuyu* (1978, first published in 1938), he criticized Europeans and missionary societies for seeking to eradicate FGC without truly understanding the practice. He disparagingly described how several European delegates to a conference on African children in 1931 referred to FGC as a "barbarous" and "heathen" custom that should be criminalized. He agreed with the majority of the conference participants, who thought providing education and free choice to the Gikuyu was the preferred course of action.

Although Kenyatta's primary argument was that Europeans should not be involved in local African social traditions, he also went on to exalt FGC as "the very essence of an institution which has enormous educational, social, moral, and religious implications" (Kenyatta 1978, 133). Both male and female circumcision occurred at puberty among the Gikuyu. Kenyatta's account of FGC minimized the physical hardship:

> The initiates spend about half an hour in the [cold] river, in order to numb their limbs and to prevent pain or loss of blood at the time of the operation . . . A woman specialist, known as *moruithia*, who has studied this form of surgery from childhood, dashes out of the crowd . . . She takes out from her pocket (*mondo*) the operating Gikuyu razor (*rwenji*), and in quick movements, and with the dexterity of a Harley Street surgeon, proceeds to operate on the

girls. With a stroke she cuts off the tip of the clitoris (*rong'otho*) . . .
At the time of the surgical operation the girl hardly feels any pain
for the simple reason that her limbs have been numbed, and the
operation is over before she is conscious of it. It is only when she
awakes after three or four hours of rest that she begins to realize
that something has been done to her genital organ (Kenyatta 1978,
143, 146, 147).

In part because of Kenyatta, the attempt to eradicate FGC among
Christian converts in Kenya was temporarily abandoned.

Although most of the world was completely unaware of FGC rituals
at mid-century, knowledge of the practice had spread outside of the
missionary community to some scholars and members of the emerging international community. The first time FGC was openly discussed
outside of Africa was in the late 1930s by the British Parliament (Murray 1976).[8] The discussion was followed initially by an informal coalition to eradicate FGC between the wives of British officials in Sudan
and educated Sudanese men. In 1943, the British launched a formal
education campaign in Sudan, and in 1946, the colonial government
passed a law forbidding the most extreme form of FGC, infibulation.
As with earlier efforts in Kenya, the law once again politicized the
issue and, rather than reducing the practice, led to the collective and
secret circumcision of many girls in a short period (El Dareer 1982,
94–95; Dorkenoo 1995).

Opposition to FGC waned in the late 1950s as African politics began to focus more on independence and nationalism. Up to this point,
eradication efforts had had little effect on rates of FGC (Assaad 1980;
Keck and Sikkink 1998). The temporary "shelving" of opposition coincided with the globalization of the nation-state system and a rise in
international interest in FGC (Berkovitch 1999a).

. . . .

THREE

The Evolution of Debates
over Female Genital Cutting

The medically correct term is "female genital mutilation."
—*Fran Hosken, "Female Genital Mutilation in the World Today," 1981*

In 1958, the Economic and Social Council of the United Nations formally requested that the World Health Organization (WHO) study
FGC. WHO refused, claiming the practice was outside the organization's competence because it was of a "social and cultural rather than
medical nature" (United Nations Yearbook 1959, 205). Three years
later, African women attending a U.N. seminar in Addis Ababa re-
iterated the request to study FGC, but WHO's response was the same
(Boulware-Miller 1985). The organization had a policy of not intervening in domestic politics without an explicit invitation from a state,
and invitations were not forthcoming.

By the mid-1990s, the situation had changed completely. The international community was centrally involved in eradicating FGC. Amnesty International included private abuses in its annual country
reports for the first time, specifically referring to the practice. The
International Monetary Fund and the World Bank (with impetus from
the United States) linked aid to reform efforts. Four other prominent
international governmental organizations (IGOs, including WHO)
issued a joint statement condemning the practice as a violation of
women's rights. In a short span of decades, the ancient practice of
FGC had become the target of unified international action. How did
this change come about?

The central premise of this chapter is that conflict between institutionalized principles creates space for this type of international reform. The chapter identifies and explains the critical turning points

in international opinion about FGC. Fundamentally, this is a story of individual rights discourse conquering first national autonomy and then family inviolability. Switchbacks and reversals play an important role in the story; key arguments rejected in one period tend to reappear and persuade in later periods.[1] The case provides evidence that individualistic frames, such as the promotion of human rights, have taken special precedence in the modern world. This does not mean that national autonomy and family autonomy disappear; rather, these structures are reshaped in relation to the dominating individualistic discourse.

Because institutions develop over eons of history and tend to be taken for granted, they impose a certain amount of inertia on society. Rather than eliminating change, however, they frame the nature of change. There are a number of examples of this in the world today. The form of change that I will focus on here is the constant expansion of individual rights and claims. As change is currently institutionalized, it is nearly impossible to make a legitimate claim to *retract* an individual right. For instance, it is hard to imagine global support for movements opposing women's right to vote, African-Americans' right to own property, or children's right to education. On the other hand, compared to such retractions, it is relatively easy to imagine support for new rights. Consider the ability of individuals to bring claims in international forums such as the European Court of Human Rights (where for many years only states could bring claims). Consider also the recent success of movements to give women greater representation in politics or gays the right to marry. Although these latter reforms have not yet been institutionalized, it is not difficult to imagine that they will be at some point. Change does not occur randomly in the international system: change explicitly calling for a revocation of rights is illegitimate; change calling for an expansion of rights is more likely to meet with success.

In this chapter, I argue that there are important consequences to the expansion of individual rights and claims—consequences illustrated by the case of FGC. The first important consequence is that change tends to undercut the authority of collective organizations such as nations and families. The second consequence is that, over time, change transforms collective organizations. Although these organizations were at one time imagined to act primarily on their own, they are increasingly called upon to act on behalf of or to facilitate the direct action of individuals. My argument is not that collective organizations are disappearing as a result of the expansion of rights but that their continuation becomes linked to an ideology of service to individuals rather than their value as entities in their own right (compare Giddens 1992). The final point of this chapter is that change in the modern system reifies the idea that individuals are the key actors in society, laying the groundwork for even more change consistent with that idea. This feeds back into the institutionalized nature of change noted above; widescale changes tend to expand rather than revoke individual claims.

Below, I illustrate how the expansion of rights was accomplished in the case of FGC. I begin with a history of the key institutional contradiction between human rights and sovereign autonomy. I then demonstrate how a health discourse provided a compromise that promoted international intervention seemingly without undermining sovereignty. Eventually, the health compromise proved inadequate as a basis for eliminating FGC. At that point, the compromise that had already been implemented facilitated the expansion of intervention. I conclude the chapter by reflecting on the implications of this outcome for the international institutions of "nation-state" and "family."

Human Rights and Sovereign Autonomy

The concept of sovereignty is closely tied to the development of the modern nation-state. A "sovereign" state is one independent of outside influence. A "sovereign" state claims the autonomous right to regulate its economy and the social life of its people. No other nation has the right to intervene in its domestic sphere.

Initially, sovereigns were kings and their legitimacy rested on their connection to a higher being. Over time, the notion of sovereignty was secularized and became lodged in state governments (see Jackson and James 1993). Under the secularized idea, the authority of state leaders was derived from the people they ruled. Through a "social contract," these individuals gave up some of their personal autonomy and entrusted it in their leaders. There was thus some expectation that these leaders would reflect the values and interests of the individuals they ruled. The resulting tension faced by political leaders —between appealing to a local constituency and reflecting higher principles (now secularized)—continues to permeate national politics. Indeed, this tension is clearly present when states adopt policies opposing FGC even though the local population supports the practice.

Sovereignty, as an ideal, is now institutionalized in the international system. The preamble to the United Nations Charter explicitly recognizes the sovereign power of member states: "Nothing contained in the present Charter shall authorize the United Nations to intervene in matters which are essentially within the domestic jurisdiction of any state." Social and cultural matters—including gender relations—were considered domestic matters at the time the charter was written (Berkovitch 1999b). For decades, the belief that cultural matters were domestic matters foreclosed international intervention to eradicate FGC.

The same Enlightenment ideas that linked states to their subjects, and later their citizens, led to the promotion of human rights. As Beccaria wrote in 1764, "The true relations between sovereigns and their subjects . . . have been discovered . . . Such good things we owe to the productive enlightenment of this age. [This knowledge will curb] the unbounded course of ill-directed power which has continually produced a long and authorized example of the most cold-blooded barbarity." Continuing to evolve since this early discourse, human rights have become a critically important component of the international institutional structure. The Geneva Assembly codified the discourse of universal human rights in 1948 with the adoption of the Universal Declaration of Human Rights (UDHR). Along with the International Covenant on Civil Rights and Political Rights and the International Covenant on Economic, Social, and Cultural Rights, both adopted by the assembly in 1966, the UDHR is said to constitute an "international bill of rights." The UDHR focuses broadly on rights seen as essential to all humans, including the rights to health and individual autonomy, which are relevant in the discussion of FGC (Smith 1995). Since 1948, there have been several conferences further detailing the means to protect and honor the rights outlined in the UDHR.

Immediately after World War II, the international community implicitly assigned gender equality (including the practice of FGC) to the "sovereign autonomy" rather than the "human rights" frame. Although the United Nations condemned FGC as a violation of human dignity and rights to health in 1964, international organizations were unwilling to get involved in actual eradication efforts (Boulware-Miller 1985). Not only did WHO and UNICEF refuse to work to eliminate the practice; they refused to even study the incidence of FGC. Even as late as 1975, there was no discussion of FGC at the First World Conference on Women (Berkovitch and Bradley 1999, 489). The widespread view was that the practice fell outside the jurisdiction of the international system.

The Health Compromise

In the early years of the U.N. system, international intervention into local politics was highly circumscribed. The cherished right of each nation to govern its own people was heralded as nation after new nation threw off the bonds of colonialism and claimed independence. In this context, the international community defined the domestic jurisdictions of nation-states broadly. In addition, international organizations did not define FGC as a health risk at this time, perhaps because the practice was passed on "voluntarily" from generation to generation. Furthermore, the negative consequences of early attempts to eradicate the practice in Kenya and Sudan might have made members of the international community reluctant to take up the issue. These factors combined to keep the international community out of the FGC controversy in the decades following World War II.

Western feminists, including Fran Hosken, Mary Daly, and Gloria Steinem, and women's international organizations were critically important in raising international interest in the practice. (African opponents to the practice had been present for some time but had been unsuccessful at getting IGOs such as WHO involved in eradication efforts.) Initially, Western women and groups were vocal and confrontational. Advocates of sovereign autonomy continually raised the question of whether the West and international organizations should be involved in the eradication of FGC. Feminists responded by arguing that FGC was a serious problem requiring immediate international attention. Feminist mobilization in the 1970s spurred the international system to take a new look at FGC.

Early second-wave feminists argued that FGC was a tool of patriarchy and a symbol of women's subordination.[2] These feminists argued that FGC was sadistic and part of a global patriarchal conspiracy. Seeing sadism in FGC actually predates feminist mobilization. For example, in one early account, Worsley claimed that the women who performed FGC "always" did so with a "sadistic smile of delight" (1967, 687). In adopting this explanation for FGC, Western women were implicitly assuming that no one would voluntarily choose to undergo the practice. African women were portrayed as victims who made "incorrect" choices because they were burdened by patriarchy.

For example, in one of the earliest feminist accounts of FGC, Daly picked up on the theme of sadism to weave together the experiences of women around the world: "Critics from Western countries are constantly being intimidated by accusations of 'racism,' to the point of misnaming, non-naming, and not seeing these sado-rituals. The accusation of 'racism' may come from ignorance, but they serve only the interests of males, not of women. This kind of accusation and intimidation constitutes an astounding and damaging reversal, for it is clearly in the interest of Black women that feminists of all races should speak out. Moreover, it is in the interest of women of all races to see African genital mutilation in the context of planetary patriarchy, of which it is but one manifestation" (1978, 154). The assumption that self-interest drives action is clearly present. Also present, although at a more subtle level, is the assumption that action motivated by something other than self-interest (God? A sense of obligation?) is illegitimate. Likewise, Hosken argued: "Men in Africa, whether illiterates or intellectuals, know very well that they derive power from castrations of women's sexuality. It is a matter of political control. The fear of female sexuality is after all shared by men around the world" (1979, 4). Again the assumption is that women where FGC occurs would choose to act in their "obvious" self-interest but for the illegitimate power exercised over them. In this quotation, Hosken is also implicitly impugning the idea of sovereign autonomy by arguing that states where FGC occurs are not representative democracies because they do not consider women's interests. Her proposed solution is apparently to provide women with a greater voice both locally and internationally. Eventually, these scathing criticisms of FGC captured the attention of international actors.

Many African women found the discourse offensive. For example, at the international women's conference in Copenhagen in 1980, African women boycotted the session featuring Fran Hosken, calling her perspective ethnocentric and insensitive to African women (Kouba and Muasher 1985). Often, individuals in cultures where FGC is practiced were offended by their characterization in anti-FGC discourse. Seble Dawit and Salem Mekuria criticized Alice Walker for failing to treat African women as efficacious and self-aware individuals: she "portrays an African village, where women and children are without personality, dancing and gazing blankly through some stranger's script of their lives" (1993, A27). Occasionally these individuals claimed that anti-FGC rhetoric was exaggerated, but more typically they argued that African women were not assigned the attributes of modern individuals. In other words, they were not assumed to be self-directed, autonomous, and efficacious.

Feminist arguments were also criticized for being ineffective at the local level. Melissa Parker, who lived with a tribe in Sudan while conducting medical research, argued that this type of discourse was doomed to fail locally:

Of course women do not circumcise their daughters to create problems for them later on. They do so to protect them. An uncircumcised girl is unmarriageable and would bring undying shame to her and her family. People would call her *kaaba* (bad), *waskhan* (dirty) and *nigsa* (unclean). Her life would be intolerable, as she would be taunted by friends and relatives wherever she went. In brief, the practice of circumcision is bound up with beliefs of honour, shame, purity and cleanliness. It is these beliefs which need to be examined and interrogated if any headway is to be made in bringing an end to such a custom. It seems almost comical that Western and Sudanese feminists have spent so much time tackling it simply at the level of female oppression when it is rooted in so much else as far as those women who experience it are concerned. (1995, 510)

Parker's perspective was essentially acknowledging that FGC was institutionalized in some areas. In these areas, history could not be ignored and "interests" had to be understood as including not only those defined by "universal" standards but also those important to the local context.

Despite the criticism, the feminist rhetoric captured the attention of the global community. By 1979, U.N. subcommittees had begun to study and provide outlets for national governments to discuss FGC. This occurred despite explicit opposition from some women in practicing cultures (Berkovitch and Bradley 1999). Nevertheless, perhaps because the feminist rhetoric was so controversial, when IGOs finally decided to intervene to stop FGC around this time, they did not explicitly rely on the feminists' arguments.

Instead, IGOs relied on scientific arguments about women's health to justify their initial intervention to eradicate FGC. WHO and nongovernmental organizations were already intervening in national arenas to assist in birth control programs (Ezzat 1994, 165–67). Programs to eliminate FGC fit well within this mobilization. For example, international actors placed FGC in a category termed Traditional Practices Affecting the Health of Women and Children (Slack 1988; Smith 1992). This was also the title given to a 1979 WHO seminar held in Khartoum and the term used to describe FGC in the U.N. annual reports. African nation-states also tended to root their eradication policies in a scientific health discourse. The major joint effort of nations was named the Inter-African Committee on Traditional Practices Affecting the Health of Women and Children. Health problems were a universal concern, affecting every nation. By placing FGC within this framework, international actors did not appear to be singling out African nations for reform. Health rhetoric permitted a compromise between rights and sovereignty.

Thus, FGC became a health issue despite WHO's early assessment that it was not. This reframing of the practice may reflect the increasing importance assigned to medicine (and science in general) in the international system. Because health issues were universally applicable to all nation-states and yet narrowly tailored to easily identifiable "problems," they were viewed as apolitical. Intervening for medical reasons did not threaten sovereignty because medicine was seen as neutral and existing apart from politics. Further, medicine was intimately linked with modernization and progress. It would be irrational and hence inconceivable for a culture to reject modern medicine.

Of course, medicine is not apolitical. Expanding notions of health to include practices like FGC privileges international politics over national sentiments and leads to isomorphism in national action. Furthermore, Western medicine is based on an individualistic model; it assumes that health problems arise from the individual body and should be treated individually. In some cases this is correct, but in other cases it is not. For example, a huge number of health problems diagnosed in the West today fall into the category of "stress-related" illnesses. Presumably, these ailments arise because individuals are having difficulty dealing with various elements of their world, including work, spouse, children, and neighbors. But medicine has no legitimate authority to address the root cause of such problems. It is highly unlikely, for example, that a doctor would call an employer or a next-door neighbor to help solve a person's medical problem. In other cultures, however, these relational ailments can become the major focus of healing strategies (see Fadiman 1997). Western medicine is founded on two important assumptions: (1) that focusing on isolated, independent individuals is the way to solve problems; and (2) that this first principle is universally true.

Thus, the fact that Western medicine has been deemed neutral and apolitical when in fact it is not reflects the expansion of universal human rights and individualism in the global system. The redefinition of FGC as a medical problem subject to "neutral" intervention simply occurred, without debate or explicit acknowledgment.

Initially, feminists were willing to reframe their arguments in the terms adopted by IGOs. Themes of human rights and medicine began to appear in the feminist literature. For example, in her 1981 report, Hosken reframed her arguments justifying Western involvement, locating them in notions of human rights and health. She cited a letter she had sent to the secretary-general of the United Nations, Kurt Waldheim, which had been signed by "many thousands of concerned women and men from all over the world": "The mutilation of genital organs of the female body for any reason whatsoever is a fundamental offense against the human rights of all women in general, and specifically against the female children and women who are muti-lated. The RIGHT TO HEALTH is a basic human right that cannot be abridged" (1981, 489, emphasis in original). (Ironically, even the "neutral" medical discourse became the basis for distinguishing a hierarchy of values. For example, Hosken [1981, 415, fn. 1] asserted in the same report that although Africans continued to call the prac-tice "female circumcision," the "medically correct" term was "genital mutilation.") In the 1980s, feminists and other international actors reached consensus through an implicit agreement to focus on the medical consequences of FGC.[3] FGC was a violation of the right to health, and therefore it was appropriate for the international com-munity to intervene in local politics to reduce the occurrence of the practice.

In sum, radical feminists prompted the international community to take action against FGC. Realizing that they must act but unwill-ing to embrace the caustic feminist discourse, community leaders had difficulty developing their own justification for intervention. Science, in the form of medicine, became a seemingly neutral basis for in-voking the human rights frame and intervening in national politics. In fact, however, the worldwide adoption of this perspective without debate was a monumental step toward global homogeneity. Individu-alism carried through medical science was acceptable to international actors; individualism in the form of assertive arguments about gen-der relationships smacked of bias and was initially too provocative for these same actors.

Women's Rights as Human Rights

Once adopted, medical arguments were the sole basis for interna-tional intervention against FGC until 1990 (WHO, UNICEF, U.N. Fam-ily Planning Association (UNFPA), and U.N. Development Program (UNDP) 1995; U.N. Population Fund 1996).[4] A number of medical organizations were at the forefront of mobilization, including WHO, the Sudanese Obstetrical and Gynecological Society, International Planned Parenthood Federation, the International Organization of Gynecologists, and Doctors without Borders (Boulware-Miller 1985). Thus, from the late 1960s until 1990, the primary goal of international organizations was to reduce the negative health consequences of the practice.

A review of the literature suggests that the medical discourse was somewhat effective in making individuals aware of health problems associated with FGC. For example, Demographic and Health Survey data show that in Kenya only 31 percent of circumcised women aged forty-five to forty-nine were circumcised by trained medical personnel, but 57 percent of circumcised women aged twenty to twenty-nine were (National Council for Population and Development 1999). Likewise, only 9 percent of Egyptian women aged forty-five to forty-nine were circumcised by trained medical personal, but 50 percent of those women had their daughters circumcised by trained medical personnel (El-Zanaty et al. 1996). This trend is not universal, however. In some countries, such as Mali and Tanzania, medicalization has been, and continues to be, minimal (Enquête Démographique et de Santé du Mali 1995–96; Bureau of Statistics 1997). Ethnographies suggest more subtle forms of medicalization as well—changes that might not be picked up in official statistics. For example, over time, ethnographies increasingly refer to the use of antiseptics to clean the wound after FGC (see, e.g., Parker 1995; Gruenbaum 2001). Regardless of whether the medical discourse actually reduced the incidence of FGC, in many areas it had the overall favorable effect of making the procedure medically safer.

Given the success of the medical mobilization against FGC, it is easy to imagine mobilization around the practice diminishing. This did not happen. Instead, mobilization increased in the 1990s—but under a rights model rather than a medical model.

Although the international community in the postwar era had been hesitant to address gender issues, a relationship between gender equality and human rights had been developing; gender equality was becoming an appropriate basis for international action. In the 1950s, 1960s, and 1970s, the United Nations and its various subunits proposed many conventions and declarations relating to gender and human rights. (Conventions are binding for the states that have ratified them; declarations are nonbinding statements of aspirations.) During this time, women came to be defined less in terms of their familial role as mothers and more in terms of their rights as individuals (Berkovitch 1999b). Most countries in the modern world have signaled their receptivity to these various conventions and declarations. The conventions and declarations provide a backdrop for understanding the policy development related specifically to FGC.

Thus, the increased attention to FGC coincided with greater attention to women's issues in general. The international system had begun to create formal mechanisms for dealing with gender inequality around this time. The Convention for the Elimination of All Forms of Discrimination against Women (CEDAW) is a case in point.[5] The history of CEDAW goes back to 1963, when twenty-two countries introduced a resolution at the eighteenth U.N. General Assembly calling for international cooperation to eliminate discrimination against women (Fraser, n.d.). The resolution noted that discrimination against women still existed "in fact if not in law" despite the equality provision of the U.N. Charter and the UDHR (United Nations 1963). On December 18, 1979, the CEDAW Convention was adopted by the General Assembly, and it came into force on September 3, 1981, when twenty countries had ratified it. As of June 2002, 170 countries had ratified the convention. Within the international treaty system, CEDAW stands distinctly as the symbol that women's rights are human rights.

The preamble to CEDAW reaffirms faith in fundamental human rights and respect for human dignity. Article 1 defines discrimination against women broadly to include both intentional and de facto discrimination in human rights and fundamental freedoms. Article 2 mandates that states parties[6] pursue, "by all appropriate means and without delay," a policy of eliminating discrimination against women. Articles 2 through 5 set out the kind of measures to be taken by the state-legislative, judicial, administrative, and other measures, including affirmative action and modification of social and cultural patterns of conduct. Articles 6 through 16 address specific issues as they relate to women: sexual slavery, political and public life, nationality, education, employment, health care, economic and social life, rural life, equality in terms of civil law, and marriage and family relations.

Like other human rights treaties, CEDAW relies on a reporting mechanism as the key to implementation. State parties have an obligation to submit written reports on the progress made in implementing CEDAW. The reports must be submitted within the first year of ratification and then periodically every four years. The convention establishes the Committee on the Elimination of All Forms of Discrimination against Women (the CEDAW Committee) to review country reports. The CEDAW Committee is composed of twenty-three experts who are nominated and elected by the state parties to serve in their personal capacities.

A number of regional instruments also provide a foundation for state mobilization against FGC (Smith 1995). For example, the African Charter on Human Rights and People's Rights and the Charter on the Rights and Welfare of the African Child contain language that justifies action against FGC. As with CEDAW, the charters do not explicitly discuss the practice but can be construed as applicable to the issue.

By the mid-1990s, feminist arguments concerning women's rights as human rights and violence against women became the dominant basis for action by IGOs. A critical component of the feminist argument was to expand the idea of human rights to incorporate a positive requirement on states to protect individuals against harmful actions that occur in the "private" realm. MacKinnon argued that the privacy doctrine undermined gender equality generally: "The very place (home, body), relations (sexual), activities (intercourse and reproduction), and feelings (intimacy, selfhood) that feminism finds central to women's subjection form the core of the privacy doctrine. But when women are segregated in private, one at a time, a law of privacy will tend to protect the right of men 'to be let alone,' to oppress us one at a time" (1983, 194). This laid the groundwork for later arguments that the idea of human rights should be expanded to encompass private abuses (see especially Bunch 1990; Bahar 1996; Charlesworth 1995; Stevens 1996).

Once "privacy" became contested terrain, human rights activists were able to transcend cultural boundaries by grouping a number of private actions and practices under the broad title "violence against women" (Bunch 1990).[7] At the international level, activists who promoted this idea were successful in increasing attention to issues such as FGC, wife beating, marital rape, child abuse, and sexual harassment (Etienne 1995; see generally Peters and Wolper 1995; Dallmeyer

1993; Cook 1994). For example, Coomaraswamy (1999) argued for a change in international law to recognize state responsibilities in the sphere of women's rights. The goal of organizing around the theme of violence against women was to focus on the common experiences of women rather than their national, racial, ethnic, or class differences (Keck and Sikkink 1998, 184).

At the same time that IGOs were beginning to see private violence as a public matter, human rights organizations were also moving in that direction. A number of feminists authored treatises arguing that women's rights are human rights. Bahar (1996) specifically criticized Amnesty International for failing to include private abuses within its working definition of human rights. Responding to this criticism, Amnesty International, which had included private abuses in its annual country reports for the first time in 1994, has continued to call for the expansion of those rights. All types of international organizations—both governmental and nongovernmental—were beginning to think expansively about the state's role in family relations. Feminist arguments that the state was responsible for protecting women and children from abuses suffered in the private sphere, arguments rejected in the 1980s, now became part of the overriding ideology of international organizations.

FGC was featured prominently among these "new" human rights abuses, and feminists also began to pressure states directly about the practice. Dorothy Stetson (1995) suggested that governments in countries where FGC occurred represented only male interests. Priscilla Warren stated the case even more strongly: "Often the victim's own government cannot or will not control the perpetrator; the state then also becomes a perpetrator" (1994, 283). Ultimately, national governments succumbed to the pressure. This is evident, for example, in the Egyptian state's abrupt turnaround on the practice. In its 1996 report to the CEDAW Committee, the Egyptian state implicitly acknowledged its responsibility in the fight against FGC (United Nations 1996, x).

By the mid-1990s, the transition from a medical model to a human rights model was complete. The FGC issue skipped from committee to committee in the organization, assigned first to a committee dealing with slavery, then moving on to a committee dealing with discrimination. Ultimately, the issue settled within the jurisdiction of the committee responsible for protecting human rights. By the time the issue reached the committee on human rights, the framing was complete: the international community had to eradicate FGC because the practice violated fundamental human rights. FGC offended the institutionalized construction of individuals as efficacious promoters of their own self-interest.

In even more dramatic terms, the joint statement of WHO, UNICEF, UNFPA, and UNDP in 1995 labeled the medical basis for anti-FGC policies a "mistake." The reasoning of the joint statement suggested that much of the medical discourse—at least as it was applied locally—was exaggerated and consequently counterproductive. The second problem with the medical reasoning was more surprising. Essentially, medicalization had been *too* effective. By making FGC safer, the international community had undermined the urgency that originally motivated the eradication of the practice. The organizations attempted to recapture some of that urgency in their repackaged message: FGC had negative health consequences, but—more importantly—it was a violation of women's rights.

Thus, in the mid-1990s, responsibility for eradicating FGC was once again reassessed. At that time, the right to health took a backseat to the human right to be free from abuse—including abuse from intimates.

The Effect of Changing Discourses

The direction of feminist mobilization had two important effects. The first was to move the international community away from the health discourse that had provided a "neutral" basis for intervention in the 1970s and 1980s, back to the gender oppression discourse that had originally been viewed as untenable. The joint statement from WHO, UNICEF, UNFPA, and UNDP was issued in draft form in 1995 and finalized in 1996. The statement critiqued prior eradication efforts for overemphasizing the medical discourse and concluded that future actions should be framed in terms of women's rights as humans.

These four IGOs turned to the repackaged feminist discourse not only because it was less threatening to cultural autonomy (being phrased even more universally than the original health discourse) but also because the medical discourse had resulted in the medicalization rather than the elimination of FGC in some areas. Specifically, the health discourse had led some individuals to suggest that milder forms of circumcision carried out under sterile conditions would be acceptable. By adopting the theme of women's rights as human rights, the IGOs were able to undermine any trends other than eradication of the practice altogether.

The second effect directly illustrates a conundrum identified by many feminists. By assigning responsibility for eradication to nation-states, asking them to intervene on women's behalf in the private sphere, the repackaged feminist discourse affirmed sovereign authority. By shaming states into intervening, feminists had provided more power to key participants in what had previously been characterized as a worldwide patriarchal system.

Although national *autonomy* was eroded by health interventions, national *power* may have actually increased as nation-states began to take responsibility for issues previously outside of their purview. The traditional distinction between public and private spheres initially made states unwilling to directly intervene to end FGC. The practice was seen as a personal family matter. Despite the attention to FGC in the 1980s, neither national governments nor the United Nations perceived states as central players in eradication efforts. Opponents of FGC had to argue not only that sovereign autonomy was no impediment to anti-FGC intervention but also that the idea of human rights encompasses abuses occurring in the private sphere. If the 1980s resulted in a subtle shift away from state autonomy toward universal individualism, then the 1990s reflected the same trend with respect to intervention into the family.

Like CEDAW, the Convention for the Rights of the Child (CRC) called for state intervention in the private sphere. The CRC was an important formal basis for FGC eradication efforts. The declaratory precursor to the CRC, which promoted children's healthy and "normal" development, was adopted by the United Nations in 1959. The

CRC, adopted in 1989, was more specific than the declaration, stating, "States Parties shall take all effective and appropriate measures with a view to abolishing traditional practices affecting women and children" (Section 24(3)). When the CRC was drafted, representatives from Italy and the Netherlands requested that Section 24(3) specifically reference FGC. The representative from Senegal argued that the language should remain general so that the provision would apply to all countries—not only African countries (Smith 1995). Although the more general language was used, the implications of the provision for eradicating FGC were clear to all state parties. The CRC also included provisions that target child abuse and the torturing of children. As with CEDAW, the CRC created a committee that assesses periodic reports of the state parties to the convention.

The motivation of this discourse was *not* to dismantle the family. Nevertheless, what a family could do—and importantly, could not do—was becoming institutionalized in a manner consistent with the tenets of individualism. The idea was emerging that in a "proper" family each *person*—each man, woman, or child—should be an equal partner. According to this ideal, it is inappropriate to view families as a convenient amalgamation of individuals linked primarily to the regulation of physical and social reproduction; the "true" purpose of every family is to provide support and love for each member. Once again, the controversy over FGC had prompted a radical change in an institution—this time, the institution of the family.

The global institutional system is always changing. One key aspect of this change is an ever-expanding notion of rights; as new claims emerge, the system expands to absorb them (Boyle and Meyer 1998). This is a contested process, however, because the expansion of individual rights tends to undercut other institutionalized arrangements. Many have noted the effect on nation-states, some even predicting the eventual demise of national sovereignty as a result of increasing economic interpenetration and international human rights intervention.[8] Rationalism and individualism—as more diffuse, symbolic concepts—tend to win out over concrete structural arrangements (state, family).

The case of FGC provides an important example of how the expansion of rights operates. Mobilization against the practice did indeed undercut national autonomy but may have increased national authority in some countries. It expanded state jurisdiction over family relationships. Although states have lost autonomy—the justification for intervening in families is standardized globally—they have gained authority vis à vis their local populations. The mantra that "the private is political" is now taken very seriously, not only in the case of FGC but for many other issues as well.

The nation and the family are now seen as important sites for the repression of individuals and hence violations of human rights. This evolving individualistic model of the nation and the family contrasts dramatically with models that existed during earlier historical eras and still exist in some locations today. These contrasting models assume that individuals exist to serve their nations and families: the primary role of the nation is to preserve a national culture against external threats, and the primary role of the family is to aid in this social reproduction (to pass down important aspects of culture from one generation to the next). Viewed from this perspective, neither the nation nor the family exists simply to please individual members.

The model of the family that is currently carried by the international system treats the personal fulfillment of individual family members as a top priority. Giddens (1992) labels this the "democratization" of personal life. This model has led to the establishment of international law to protect both women and children from the consequences of unequal power in the family. The complementary model of the nation-state has led to tremendous isomorphism in national policies.

Will the family ultimately become a "global" institution, subject to the same homogenizing processes that nation-states currently experience? This question is important but much too complex to answer here. Suffice it to say that FGC and other issues capturing the attention of international actors today certainly suggest that the family may be the current site for expanding universal individualism.

With respect to both the nation-state and the family, being constituted by the global system does not spell demise. Nation-states will not disappear as a consequence of increasing attention to human rights.

They are necessary to move the projects of modernity and individualism forward. Families will not disappear as a consequence of international attempts to equalize their internal power relationships. Rather than disappearing, organizations constituted by and within global institutions may lose autonomy and become rather standardized repositories of institutional principles.

FOUR

International Mobilization

Teamwork must bring together government, political and religious institutions, international organizations, nongovernmental organizations, and funding agencies in their efforts to eliminate this harmful practice.
—*World Health Organization, Female Genital Mutilation (1997)*

Letters in my correspondence file perhaps best illustrate the different early positions of international organizations on the issue of FGC. In 1998, I had just begun to study the issue. My research assistant, Mayra Gómez, and I sent letters to a long list of international organizations asking for any information they had on anti-FGC programs. In our letters, we referred to the practice as "female genital mutilation." Among the responses was a letter from the U.S. Agency for International Development (USAID).[1] The letter, written by Asma Abdel Halim, suggested that we use the term "female genital cutting" because the USAID Task Force on the issue had found "female genital cutting" to be "less pejorative" and "better received by the communities that practice the procedure." This state-sponsored organization implicitly acknowledged disagreements between Americans and at least some Africans. Further, the organization was clearly concerned about alienating African women.

Two years later, Mayra and I wanted to share some of the results of our research with the organizations that had generously sent us information. Once again, we sent a mailing to all of the organizations on our list. This time we used the term "female genital cutting." Once again, many organizations replied. This time, the cover letter from the Women's International Network (WIN) targeted our terminology. The letter said that women in Africa had never heard of "female genital cutting" and that the appropriate term was "female genital muti-lation." WIN is a private organization established by Fran Hosken to address gender inequality throughout the world. It specifically tar-gets FGC. In contrast to the letter from USAID, this letter wanted to promote the idea that all women—whether American or African—agreed unequivocally with the condemnation of FGC.

International organizations in recent years have been consistent in their desire to eradicate FGC. Nevertheless, as these two letters sug-gest, different organizations adopted different perspectives in their efforts to accomplish that goal. My argument is that the unique roles played by different types of organizations in the international sys-tem interact with important principles to produce predictable vari-ation in organizational strategies. The implication is that organiza-tions linked into the current power arrangement (the sovereignty system) are likely to be more cautious and deferential than other orga-nizations. This argument runs parallel to my argument in chapter 8 that the structural location or local cultural milieu of individuals in-fluences the basis by which they explain their opposition to FGC.

Over time, as the eradication of FGC has become a taken-for-granted goal of the international system, the strategies have begun to look similar. Nongovernmental organizations (NGOs) began the period with highly critical rhetoric but tended to tone down their lan-guage over time (with the possible exception of WIN). State-spon-sored organizations operated more timidly at first but became more assertive over time. To continue with the example of terminology, today many state-sponsored organizations use the term "mutilation" and many private organizations use the term "cutting." One NGO, Equality Now, indicates that it will not judge contributions to its Web site by the term used to describe FGC. Nevertheless, the two letters do illustrate a pattern of differences that was important in the early stages of anti-FGC mobilization.

What is it about organizations and their contexts that caused them to adopt distinctly different anti-FGC strategies? It seems that organi-zations' connection to the state sovereignty system is one important factor. Specifically, the structural location of actors in the interna-tional system appears to be closely linked to the anti-FGC strategies they adopt; the greater their dependence on the sovereignty system, the more deference they give to local culture and politics. The contrasting letters from USAID and WIN illustrate this difference. In general, the approach of state-sponsored organizations started out being more assimilative, while the approach of private NGOs started out being more confrontational. Once their cause become globally recognized, the strategic differences become less pronounced.

International Actors

The most privileged entity in the modern international system is the state. States are the implementers of policy. Their purposive action takes center stage in the international arena (Boyle and Meyer 1998). States have taxing power and therefore key resources. But along with privilege comes responsibility. States are under pressure to demonstrate their commitment to international ideals. Because they hold key resources, states are frequently the focus of inter- and intranational mobilization (Keck and Sikkink 1998). However, because states must pay for new policies and deal with intranational groups that oppose change, they are slower to act than other international actors (Meyer and Jepperson 2000). Further, states adopt policies but may decouple those policies from action and buffer local populations from the changes. Nation-states are linked to international norms, but because they are concretely responsible for reform and must deal with reactions to reform, they tend to be cautious.

The state's privileged status in the international system has led some to treat it as the only relevant unit in international relations. Numerous scholars have pointed out the inaccuracies of such a perspective (see, e.g., Boli and Thomas 1999a; Keck and Sikkink 1998; Price 1997). States exist within a global society that legitimates their existence and influences their actions (Boli 1999; Thomas and Meyer 1984). The many characteristics that very different states share are evidence of the importance of international norms in creating state identity (Finnemore 1996). Other international actors, including international governmental organizations (IGOs) and NGOs, are important members of the global community as well.

IGOs (such as the U.N.) are very influential in shaping state action around the globe (Boli and Thomas 1999b; McNeely 1995; Barnett and Finnemore 1999). IGOs are not reducible to independent state interests, but unlike NGOs, IGOs *are* dependent on the sovereignty system for their existence. If there were no nation-states, there would be no IGOs. Consequently, although IGOs may be sympathetic to many types of principled ideas, the principled idea of sovereign autonomy carries particular weight for IGOs and limits the intrusiveness of their reform strategies. In essence, the criticisms and strategies of IGOs are constrained by their dependence on the sovereignty system. When issues of sovereign autonomy are involved, IGOs avoid hasty action. For example, the Sub-Committee on the Prevention of Discrimination and Protection of Minorities (one of the first IGOs to take action against FGC) took two years (1982–84) to study and discuss whether to take action against FGC. IGOs push for reform but are sympathetic to nation-states' desire to act cautiously.

NGOs (such as WIN and Amnesty International) derive their authority from scientific and moral claims institutionalized in the global system.[2] Their authority is based largely on the legitimacy of their causes; they incorporate the prevailing model of the individual and the logic of authority based on sovereignty into their rhetoric. Their legitimacy is enhanced by their frequent rejection of self-interest in the name of more collective goods.

Such sources of authority endow them with identities that are universal and transcend national borders. Their continued existence does not depend on sovereignty (Meyer and Jepperson 2000). Consequently, NGOs assign less importance to local culture than do either IGOs or states. They are more likely to adopt an outspoken and critical discourse in part because they are not responsible for the implementation of and have little financial accountability for the ideas they propose. Although they provide crucial information to IGOs, NGOs do politicking involving more than simply information politics. For example, NGOs enhance the legitimacy of the United Nations by showing that the United Nations is embedded among "the people." Even individuals with no formal political standing theoretically have access to the United Nations through NGOs. NGOs can also mobilize material resources for U.N. causes (e.g., the International Chamber of Commerce) or local actors. In practice, NGOs take advantage of their transnational status to establish networks both globally and locally (Keck and Sikkink 1998). They exist in a mutually dependent relationship with IGOs.

Neither IGOs nor NGOs have coercive power in the Weberian sense (Franck 1990). This does not mean that IGOs have no independent authority, however. IGOs', NGOs', and nation-states' legitimacy is interdependent. The legitimacy of all is boosted when they demonstrate that their projects concur on important principles (Barrett and Frank 1999). All lose legitimacy when they fail to demonstrate that nation-states are mostly linked to the "natural order" of the international system (cf. Edelman, Uggen, and Erlanger 1999). This may explain why their strategies to eradicate FGC became more similar after they had succeeded in capturing the attention of an international audience.

Their initial strategies were notably different from one another. The structural factors just described influenced IGOs to defer to nation-states in their mobilization against FGC. NGOs, operating outside the formal constraints of the nation-state system, adopted contrary strategies. While IGOs initially sought to cajole nation-states into adopting anti-FGC policies, NGOs were more vitriolic and direct in their criticism. NGOs were more likely to characterize national governments as complicit in the continuation of FGC and with intense determination capitalized on numerous opportunities to call to task governments or other institutions that they perceived as sympathetic to FGC's continuation. NGOs, unlike IGOs, had little motivation to defer to national autonomy, so NGOs' strategies were different from IGOs' strategies.

Rounding out these contrasting action plans, the strategies of nation-states in their capacities as international actors covered a wide spectrum, from discreet modeling to outright coercion. In general, nation-states acted more like IGOs, largely deferring to local policy-making apparatuses. The powerful United States represented an exception, however. A powerful civil society in the United States fueled coercive action, while bureaucratic organizations within the state structure itself were more cautious. The United States adopted a full range of strategies—sometimes attempting to assimilate local communities into reform efforts but at other times adopting a punitive strategy to motivate reform.

Ultimately, the diverse strategies of IGOs, NGOs, and states prompted policy reform around the world. This chapter details the actions of particular segments of the international community, starting with IGOs, moving next to NGOs, then to the media, and finally to states. Throughout the chapter, the analysis links the dominance of certain principled ideas to the form of eradication efforts, explaining how the strategies of international actors were driven by their differing structural locations in the international system.

International Community Action

When the international community first took up the issue of FGC in the early 1960s, sovereign autonomy was at its peak, and there was no attempt to coordinate an eradication of the practice. The World Health Organization maintained its policy to not intervene in domestic politics without an explicit invitation from the state (El Dareer 1982). It was decades later when a wave of interest, linked closely to women's and children's human rights, prompted the international community to make FGC an international concern and to take more concrete action against the practice (Assaad 1980; Etienne 1995; Boulware-Miller 1985). The U.N. General Assembly declared 1975 the International Year of Women and 1975–85 the International Decade for Women.

Both domestic and international NGOs became very important in eradication efforts at this time. Mobilization occurred on several fronts simultaneously. In 1975, a feminist organization in Burkina Faso (then Upper Volta), Les Femmes Voltaiques, began national radio broadcasts against FGC (Boulware-Miller 1985). In Kenya and Sudan, organized opposition to the practice had never entirely disappeared after early eradication efforts, and in the 1970s, intra- and international anti-FGC organizations began to work together. For example, the Sudanese Obstetrical and Gynecological Society sponsored a local meeting to discuss FGC in 1977 (Boulware-Miller 1985).

Likewise, in Egypt, organized opponents of FGC had been around for decades but once again became linked to the international discourse at this time.

In 1978, perhaps in anticipation of the 1980 Convention for the Elimination of All Forms of Discrimination against Women (CEDAW Convention), Western groups such as Save the Children, the Féderation Internationales des Femmes de Carrières Juridiques, and Terre des Hommes sent detailed information about FGC to the secretary-general of the United Nations (Boulware-Miller 1985). In the same year, France began to prosecute cases of FGC as child abuse (Winter 1994). In 1979, Africans and non-Africans met in Khartoum, Sudan, to attend the World Health Organization–sponsored Conference on Traditional Practices Affecting the Health of Women and Children. Recommendations emanating from the Khartoum conference focused on education and on the perceived need for grassroots involvement in the movement to eradicate FGC (Smith 1995).

Reform Strategies

Gusfield (1986) notes that some of the most contentious political issues have nothing to do with individuals' economic interests; instead, they are battles over status. When particular practices distinguish members of different cultures, it becomes important to place those practices into a "hierarchy" of lifestyles. They become symbols of social status. When the dominant group feels its position is threatened, it reacts by imposing its social practices on other groups. The case of FGC is quite different from Gusfield's case (abolition) because FGC is a matter of international rather than national politics. Nevertheless, Gusfield's theory of status politics may provide some clues to explain the timing of the international community's concern about this local cultural practice.

Widespread international mobilization against FGC occurred only after countries from all continents were explicitly joined in a single "community" through the United Nations. Gusfield suggests that threats from immigrants can create the impetus for national status reform. The FGC experience suggests that the same effect might occur when previously disparate groups come to be defined as part of the same community—even if none of them actually moves physically.

According to Gusfield, status reform efforts may occur through either assimilation ("converting the sinner") or coercion (forcing compliance). Assimilative reform relies on the legitimation of the dominant values, while coercive reform requires domination. Although both strategies were employed by international actors seeking to eradicate FGC, initially IGOs tended to favor assimilative reform and NGOs were more likely to favor coercive reform.

The first of several critical events shaping the overall direction of the anti-FGC movement occurred in 1980 at the NGO conference held in parallel to the U.N. Copenhagen conference. There, African women boycotted a panel on FGC for being insensitive to African perspectives on the topic. Subsequently, the World Health Organization and UNICEF sponsored a consultative meeting in Cairo (Kouba and Muasher 1985). During the Cairo meeting, African and Asian delegates held the floor. Western members, with one exception, did not participate in the discussion. The one Westerner who did speak up was chastised.[3] This is one of the earliest explicit examples of the divergence between IGO eradication strategies, which tended to be deferential to African perspectives, and NGO eradication strategies, which tended to be more confrontational.

International Governmental Organization Strategies

Assimilative strategies of reform deferential to sovereign autonomy were explicitly adopted by IGOs such as the World Health Organization in the early 1980s. The idea of assimilative strategies is to persuade nation-states to voluntarily acquiesce to reform efforts. For example, the joint statement issued by the World Health Organization, UNICEF, the U.N. Family Planning Association (UNFPA), and the U.N. Development Program (UNDP) stated: "We must work from the assumption that human behaviours and cultural values, however senseless they may look to us from our particular personal and cultural standpoints, have meaning and fulfill a function for those who practise them. People will change their behavior only when they themselves understand the hazards and indignity of the harmful practices and perceive the new practices proposed as meaningful, functional, and at least as effective as the old ones. Therefore, what we must aim for is to convince people, including women, that they can give up a specific practice *without* giving up meaningful aspects of their own cultures" (1995, 2, emphasis in original). In general, the IGO strategies included respecting sovereign autonomy and focusing on legitimating anti-FGC mobilization and delegitimating support for FGC. Even after they decided to take action, these organizations were slower than NGOs to label FGC a human rights abuse (McLean and Graham 1985).

IGOs included African countries in international decision-making processes with respect to FGC. For example, the 1979 Khartoum conference sponsored by the World Health Organization (see above) produced recommendations focused on education and grassroots mobilization (Smith 1995). IGOs also demonstrated empathy toward African perspectives. In this regard, Egyptian doctor Nawal El Saadawi talked about her circumcision experience and spoke out against the practice at the 1980 Copenhagen conference (Kouba and Muasher 1985). As noted above, the World Health Organization and UNICEF sponsored a follow-up consultative meeting in Cairo in 1980 for the explicit purpose of incorporating the perspective of African nations into the international debate. Brennan describes how the Sub-Committee on the Prevention of Discrimination and Protection of Minorities supported "the internal African eradication efforts through education and persuasion" (1989).

The United Nations Development Fund for Women (UNIFEM) has been a particularly important source of funding for local anti-FGC organizations. In 1998, a UNIFEM Trust Fund grant of $768,000 joined U.N. agencies, an American NGO (Program for Appropriate Technology and Health [PATH]), and a Kenyan NGO (Maendeleo Ya Wanawake Organization [MYWO]) to eradicate FGC in three regions of Kenya (PATH/MYWO 1998). To illustrate the expected success of this effort, the UNIFEM Web site tells the story of Zipporah Kittony, a member of Kenya's parliament, who now works on the UNIFEM-sponsored project. Kittony ran away from home when she was thirteen to participate in a circumcision ceremony. Her parents, who objected to FGC, found her before the ceremony and took her home: "'I cried and cried,' she recalls. 'I just wanted to be like everybody else and fit in'" (UNIFEM 2002). Kittony explains that when she was older, she learned of the negative health consequences of FGC and thanked her parents for forbidding her from being circumcised. According to the UNIFEM Web site, Kittony is optimistic that MYWO will succeed in eradicating FGC.

The UNIFEM-sponsored project explicitly recognizes the symbolic value of FGC among certain communities in Kenya. Furthermore, it calls for unique programs tailored to each community's unique characteristics. For example, the project report states: "Giving the communities the opportunity to go at their own pace and to plan according to their needs was key to the success of the program," and "Answers must come from communities, and we must remember that in each one, change takes a different form."

In the village of Tharaka, rather than eliminating initiation ceremonies altogether, they devised an alternative rite of passage called Ntaniro Na Mugambo—Circumcision with Words (PATH/MYWO 1998). The aim of the project was to substitute circumcision with training on "empowerment, health, and human rights" (PATH/MYWO 1998). The project team attempted to garner support from village elders and to educate young boys about the harms of FGC.

The extent to which the project team's efforts will reduce FGC in Kenya is unknown. At the time of the project report in 1998, none of the thirty girls who were in the Circumcision with Words program had experienced FGC, and the report stated that the "bigger picture is even more promising." However, a more cautious assessment emerges from Kiyofumi Tanaka (2000) of the International Development Center of Japan, who conducted an anthropological study of the Gusii (also known as the Abagusii) ethnic group in Kenya. He accepts the PATH/MYWO assessment that the rate of FGC has decreased from 100 percent among women aged 50 or older to 78 percent among teenage girls. Nevertheless, he fears the trend away from FGC may be slowing, in part because members of MYWO are losing their resolve to oppose the practice: "Despite advocacy by MYWO and [Seventh Day Adventist—Rural Health Services], it is reported that so far only a few people in the district have stopped circumcising their daughters. What is apparently slowing down the trend towards ending the practice is the lack of openness among the anti-female genital cutting crusaders. Focus group discussion participants reported that some community leaders such as MYWO representatives, who preach against the practice, are known to take their girls for the operation secretly. This double standard attitude among the community leaders discourages community members who might like to adopt an anti-circumcision stand" (Tanaka 2000, 35). As the project's own report noted, the girls adopting the alternative rite of passage were teased and ostracized in social circles for failing to be circumcised. For this and other reasons, it is difficult for community members to resist the pressure to circumcise their daughters.

The UNIFEM-sponsored project illustrates one important assimilative strategy favored by IGOs—to encourage grassroots movements in the countries where FGC is practiced. It is not difficult to find local grassroots organizations; many existed prior to international mobilization. Cumulatively, the 1979 Khartoum conference, the 1980 Copenhagen conference, and the 1980 Cairo conference energized preexisting African women's organizations and led to the creation of new African organizations. In addition to MYWO, these organizations include the Somali Women's Development Organization, the Central African Republic Organization, Le Mouvement Femmes et Societe in Senegal, the Union National des Femmes du Mali, and the Babiker Badri Scientific Society in Sudan (Boulware-Miller 1985; Kouba and Muasher 1985). Marie Bassili Assaad and El Saadawi of Egypt; two Sudanese doctors, Asma El Dareer and Nahid Toubia; and other African women, such as Efua Dorkenoo, have written books and articles and organized educational campaigns to eradicate the practice. In sum, international actors recognized a sizable opposition to FGC within African countries around 1979, and a coalition of inter- and intranational organizations was forged.

In 1982, the United Nations began to commission studies to determine the prevalence of FGC and eradication strategies (United Nations Yearbook 1982). The World Health Organization brought Africans and Westerners together again in Dakar, Senegal, in 1984 to discuss anti-FGC policies. This seminar resulted in the creation of the splinter organization Inter-African Committee on Traditional Practices Affecting the Health of Women and Children, derived from the pre-existing Working Group on Traditional Practices Affecting Women and Children (Smith 1995, 82). Although technically an NGO, the Inter-African Committee is more closely linked to IGOs and nation-states than to other NGOs because of this background. The mandate of the Inter-African Committee was to initiate and support national committees in the African countries where FGC is practiced and to raise funds to support local opposition (Smith 1995, 53). The Inter-African Committee has since been at the forefront of anti-FGC mobilization.

The major strategies of IGOs were to study FGC and to provide outlets for national governments to discuss FGC. IGOs did not attempt to shame or coerce African governments into taking action (Brennan 1989). It is important to point out that despite the attention to the practice, neither national governments nor IGOs initially perceived national governments as central players in eradication efforts. Overall, IGOs attempted to develop an international consensus on FGC, to get nations to act of their own volition, and to increase African mobilization (Brennan 1989). NGO strategies provide a dramatic contrast.

International Nongovernmental Organization Strategies

Although eschewed by U.N. organizations, coercive reforms emanating from some international NGOs (as well as some private individuals and the United States) appeared alongside IGOs' more assimilative reforms. In general, coercive reform condemns FGC in outright terms. Alice Walker's 1992 novel, *Possessing the Secret of Joy,* would fall into this category.[4] An even more dramatic portrayal of the practice from a Nigerian NGO recently crossed my desk. The summary of the practice stated that "most often the child dies under the excruciating pain and agonizing cries in excess bleeding" accompanying FGC (Villagelife Panorama 2001, 12).

Coercive reform strategies can also include attempts to undermine the legitimacy of a state. For example, activists sometimes took the position that inactive national governments were not truly representative of their citizens (Stetson 1995). By highlighting the distance between states and local constituencies, NGOs provided a foundation for direct international intervention. Perhaps an even more common coercive strategy was the public embarrassment of inactive governments. Forcing the issue of FGC into the public in dramatic narrative forms had this effect. For example, CNN's live filming of the ten-year-old's cutting in Cairo resulted in tremendous negative publicity for the Egyptian government. NGOs simultaneously arranged a heated anti-FGC campaign. As noted before, the timing maximized the level of international attention.

The year after the CNN filming, the World Health Organization, UNICEF, UNFPA, and UNDP issued their joint statement against FGC, suggesting that the shaming strategy had captured their attention. At the same time, the United Nations bestowed the 1995 Population Award on the Inter-African Committee for its efforts in eradicating FGC. By not granting the award to the CNN film crew, the United Nations may have been attempting to distance itself from the NGOs' strategy of public humiliation. Nevertheless, the NGOs' strategy had grabbed the attention, if not the approval, of both IGOs and the Egyptian government.

Furthermore, the coercive reforms were effective. At the end of the Cairo conference, the United Nations declared: "Governments are urged to prohibit female genital mutilation wherever it exists and to give vigorous support to efforts among NGOs and community organizations and religious institutions to eliminate such practices . . . Measures should be adopted to eliminate and enforced to eliminate . . . FGM" (Smith 1995, 56).

In July 1996, Egypt filed its third periodic report to the CEDAW Committee. The change in Egypt's position since its first report six years earlier was evident. While continuing to maintain that the practice of FGC was dying out, the report acknowledged the state's responsibility for eradicating the practice. Just as the report was being filed, the Egyptian Health Minister expanded his decree to forbid any medical professional from performing female circumcisions, even in private hospitals.

Since the Copenhagen conference in 1980, coercive strategies have been criticized by a number of Africans (Obiora 1997; Dawit and Mekuria 1993). Initially, the criticisms seemed to have little effect on those deploying coercive strategies, perhaps because their strategies were effective at gaining international attention. But, over time, it appears that NGOs have cut back on their confrontational strategies.

Media Coverage

Personal stories and narratives are the true core of NGO mobilization, which links NGOs very closely to the media. The media represents a unique type of NGO; it is independent of the sovereignty system, but "neutrality" is one important basis for its legitimacy. The media sometimes engaged in coercive reform tactics but eventually settled into milder forms of criticism. Andrea Hoeschen and I (2001) analyzed twenty years of newspaper stories on FGC to get a sense of how the international media has dealt with the controversial issue.

The first newspaper coverage of FGC emerged shortly after the initial international mobilization in the late 1970s. One of the earliest stories appeared in the *New York Times* on July 18, 1980. It provided coverage of the United Nations Conference on Women in Copenhagen. It began with the dramatic narrative of Nawal El Saadawi's circumcision as a child. As noted earlier, El Saadawi had become an anti-FGC activist and was speaking in opposition to the practice at the conference. The article was thorough, beginning with the attention-getting human interest story, moving on to discuss a World Health Organization report on FGC, and finally describing the contentious debates at the Conference on Women over whether anti-FGC mobilization was imperialistic. The article was representative of others written at the same time. It was designed to evoke reader sympathies, it provided favorable coverage of powerful international actors (the United Nations and the World Health Organization), and it analyzed the competing principles of sovereign autonomy and the human right of bodily integrity. Reports of this type coincided with the emergence of international cooperation to eradicate FGC.

News coverage of the mobilization against FGC was initially quite sparse. Over time, the number of articles increased, and the articles became more specific in their purposes. Beginning in the 1990s, the number of articles on FGC steadily increased until it peaked in 1996 (the year in which the United States adopted anti-FGC legislation). A number of key events in the anti-FGC campaign occurred during this time period. The first was the release of Alice Walker's novel *Possessing the Secret of Joy* and subsequent documentary *Warrior Marks* (with Pratibha Parmar), both criticizing FGC. The novel and documentary became publicly available in 1992 and 1993, respectively. The second major event was the 1994 CNN filming of a circumcision while Egypt was hosting an International Conference on Population and Development. The third major event was the U.S. asylum case of Fauziya Kassindja in 1996. Kassindja was a nineteen-year-old native of Togo who fled her country to avoid FGC. Finally, shortly after the Kassindja case, the United States passed legislation making FGC illegal and making U.S. support for loans from international financial institutions dependent on foreign governments' carrying out educational campaigns against FGC.

Keck and Sikkink (1998) suggest that international mobilization strategies include the use of symbolism, information, leverage, and accountability. These four strategies also accurately characterize the cycle of frames for newspaper articles on FGC. Over time, articles changed from predominantly coercive to predominantly assimilative. "Symbolism" stories are equivalent to human interest stories, focusing on images or persons to humanize or individualize FGC. For example, the following excerpt is from the *Chicago Tribune*, July 18, 1993: "I knew what he was doing to me. He had given me local anesthetic to numb the area, but it didn't help. I always will hear the sound of the scissors cutting the flesh between my legs. The pain was horrendous; I struggled to get away, but was held down by three people, including my mother."[5]

Information stories describe in a scientific or expert fashion the extent to which FGC is supported and practiced and the medical consequences for women. These stories tend to be less personalized, more scientific, and more research oriented than symbolic stories. *Xinhua News Agency*, June 26, 1994, provides an example of an article using an information strategy: "The art ranges from circumcision, in which part of the clitoris is removed, to the more extreme forms of excision. The five countries where three quarters of the women mutilated in this way in Africa can be found are Ethiopia, Egypt, Sudan, Kenya, and Nigeria and it is usually carried out before the age of two or before marriage."[6]

Leverage strategies include the discussion of organized activity to obtain a policy or behavior change with respect to FGC. These strategies tend to facilitate the sense of global consensus over eradication efforts. As an example of an article using a leverage strategy, Sarah Gauch, on page 1 of the *Chicago Tribune* on September 10, 1995, described the perspective of Egyptian activists who campaigned against the practice: "Thirty-five women's rights activists, doctors, and academics formed the Female Genital Mutilation Task Force. Government officials announced legal action to curb the practice, and human rights groups began developing their own programs to stop female circumcision, frequently called female genital mutilation, to emphasize its severity compared to male circumcision."[7]

Accountability strategies also suggest principled consensus over the eradication of FGC, but in terms of completed policy actions. For example, accountability-strategy stories included articles about the adoption of formal or binding government policies on FGC (e.g., court decisions, legislation, adoption of a ban, decisions on the conduct of educational programs); any enforcement activity with respect to such policies (arrest, charges, imprisonment); and the incidence of any noncompliance with the policies. The following article, which appeared in the *Deutsche Presse-Agentur* on September 12, 1994, discusses the actions of the Egyptian state: "Egyptian authorities are questioning the Cairo crew of the American CNN television network about a film showing the circumcision of a 10-year-old Egyptian girl beamed worldwide a few days ago. Cairo press reports said that three men, including the girl's father, have been arrested for allegedly taking money from CNN to allow them to film the procedure."[8]

A reading of the articles on FGC suggests a link between activism and media coverage. The earliest articles often covered international conferences. In 1994, newspapers reported on the CNN filming. In their coverage of the incident, newspaper reports uniformly condemned the practice and disparaged the Egyptian government for its inaction.[9] Furthermore, newspapers continued to cover the story of FGC in Egypt for years after the filming, resulting in immense pressure on Egypt to undertake eradication efforts.

For example, it appears that the NGO Equality Now took advantage of the sudden media interest in FGC to begin a letter campaign to the media about the practice.[10] Several months after Egypt's limited anti-FGC policy was announced, the *New York Times* and the *Washington Post* both covered Equality Now's criticism that hospitals were performing circumcisions daily instead of once a week, that doctors were competing for opportunities to perform the procedure because of the fees involved, and that no advisory committees were present to dissuade parents against the practice.[11] Until the end of 1996, the media covered new developments in Egypt, including the progression of several lawsuits.[12] This suggests that news stories are geared toward more than simply selling newspapers or "neutrally" reporting on current events; they may also be designed to promote a cause.

Researchers tend to explain media actions in terms of coercion by powerful interest groups or rational self-interest. While these explanations of media behavior are important, our research suggested a third explanation—the institutionalized normative framework in which journalists are embedded. Beginning from this unique vantage point, our analysis of media reports demonstrated that when journalists are linked to and believe in the project they are covering, the form of their stories tends to track NGO tactics. The form of stories on FGC completed a cycle of symbolism, information, leverage, and accountability before tapering off. This pattern contrasts with the predictions of media self-interest theories: that newspaper coverage of an issue will diminish as stories become less graphic and symbolic.

Stories tended to retain a symbolic or informative element throughout the cycle of coverage but not as their primary theme. Furthermore, the interaction of leverage and accountability was fairly complex. Journalists did not simply write leverage stories for a period of time and then write accountability stories. Rather, leverage and accountability stories "traded off," in a pattern where first one and then the other dominated the news scene. Perhaps because the dramatic narratives of NGO activists were reaching more people, more people began to take the appropriateness of eradication efforts for granted. Once that happened, there were fewer news stories on proposed solutions and more news stories on success and implementation.

State Strategies

In terms of their structural location in the international system, states have taxing power and therefore key resources. They are linked into international norms but must also pay for new policies and deal with local protest groups (Meyer and Jepperson 2000). Because they are concretely responsible for reform and must deal with reactions to reform, they tend to be cautious.

Western states, perhaps in part because of the minimal cost to them, acted early in anti-FGC efforts. They were the first to adopt anti-FGC legislation in the recent period. Former colonial powers were especially well represented. In 1982, Sweden became the first Western country to adopt anti-FGC legislation. From 1982 until 1995, all of the Western laws were local; they banned the practice within national borders or indicated that local assault or child abuse statutes were applicable to the practice.

The United States was a unique case among Western countries. Actions emanating from U.S. civil society and its elected representatives were often coercive. For example, the U.S. law linked foreign aid to eradication efforts in other countries.[13] On the other hand, actions emanating from formal U.S. bureaucracies were more assimilative. The letter I received from USAID is an example of the latter. USAID's representative was clearly rejecting embarrassment as a solid basis for reform.

This may reflect the fact that the U.S. government is a relatively weak state; civil society is more central in policymaking than bureaucratic experts are. Further, American civil society operates independently of the nation-state system. Although U.S. government officials, especially those involved in international relations, may be sensitive to sovereignty issues, individuals in American civil society operate independently of the sovereignty system. Like NGOs, private American individuals are less likely to be concerned about maintaining the legitimacy of nation-states than individuals who actually have a stake in the sovereignty system. This is true not only because Americans are private citizens but also because the United States has more power than most other nation-states. Arguably, even if the U.S. government lost authority, American economic and cultural power would persist. For these reasons, U.S. anti-FGC positions were somewhat inconsistent across spheres.

Although some African states took action against FGC while still colonies or immediately after achieving independence, the vast majority adopted anti-FGC policies after Western countries did. A number of African nations were hesitant to incur the local political costs associated with criminalizing FGC. It was only when international pressure increased the cost of *not* criminalizing FGC that most African states began to adopt anti-FGC policies. I discuss this process in more detail in the next chapter.

Structural Location and Strategies of Mobilization

The different structural positions of states, IGOs, and NGOs are linked but unique, and their uniqueness shapes each entity's priorities and strategies of action. A commitment to global institutionalized principles forces the three types of international actors to take each other seriously. At the same time, the degree of dependency on the sovereignty system and political/financial accountability lead to variation in the entities' outlooks. Fundamentally, the entities exist on a continuum, with states the most dependent on sovereignty (especially relatively weak states) and facing the greatest degree of local constituent accountability. As a consequence, when one weighs the principled ideas of national autonomy and gender equality, states are the organizations that come down most firmly on the side of national autonomy. Lacking the same structural constraints, NGOs are the staunchest supporters of the principles of gender equality and individual rights.

The structural position of international organizations also patterns their global policymaking. Policies devised through the collaboration of states and IGOs would likely remain decoupled if left on their own. Surrounding this somewhat formalized exchange, however, is the less predictable and often more coercive input of NGOs. Because NGOs are less linked to the sovereignty system, they are less impressed by issues of sovereign autonomy and more outcome oriented than either IGOs or nation-states. NGOs believe that what is genuinely "good" (e.g., international norms) should be given first priority by states (Chabbott 1999). As a consequence, NGOs cause what social movement scholars refer to as "the effect of the radical flank" (McAdam, McCarthy, and Zald 1996). They make radical proposals for change and thus raise the baseline for the range of action nation-states should take. When NGOs made a convincing case for outright eradication of FGC, the Egyptian government could not remain indifferent but had to do *something* to signal commitment to change.

By contrast, states often take a more "realistic" and gradualist approach toward international norms, which often serves to disguise (or is viewed as disguising) reluctance or inability to implement change. The interaction of these major players in the international arena becomes the basis for action-oriented national reforms, the focus of the next chapter.

FIVE

The Diffusion of National Policies against Female Genital Cutting

Even if the law is not enforced or enforceable, the symbolic import of its passage is important to the reformer. It settles the controversies between those who represent clashing cultures. The public support of one conception of morality at the expense of another enhances the prestige and self-esteem of the victors and degrades the culture of the losers.
—*Joseph R. Gusfield,* Symbolic Crusade, *1986*

The U.S. State Department issues Human Rights Reports each year describing the human rights situation in many countries of the world. These reports have been available for download from the Internet for several years. At the State Department Web site, each country has its own link, which leads to the country's individualized report. Once inside a country report, the Web surfer cannot link to any other country report. Each report is unambiguously independent of all other reports. The Web site seems to reflect the State Department's operating assumption that states are fundamentally independent and act autonomously (cf. Ferguson 1994).

A closer examination of the reports reveals that even as the State Department makes an assumption of independence, the goal of the reports is to standardize action across countries. The content of the reports reflects a standardized list of issues that are cherished by Americans. No attempt is made to gauge local national polities' attitudes toward these issues. There is no acknowledgment that local individuals might find other issues equally or even more important. Each report is divided into six sections. Across countries, the six headings labeling each section are identical (e.g., Respect for Political Rights:

The Right of Citizens to Change Their Government). FGC, which first appeared in the reports in 1994, always appears in Section 5: Discrimination Based on Race, Sex, Religion, Disability, Language, or Social Status, under the subheading Children. The language describing the practice is always the same, making no attempt to capture the unique meaning assigned to the practice in different areas: "Female genital mutilation . . . is widely condemned by international health experts as damaging to both physical and psychological health." Descriptions of local reactions to the practice are only slightly less standardized. They mention the presence or absence of legal reform, education efforts, and involvement by international and local organizations. The issue of FGC, like the other standard repertoire of issues raised in these reports, is presented primarily from an American perspective.

Although every country has its own report, the implicit assumption of the State Department's Human Rights Reports is that all countries do or should share American values and priorities. This is hardly surprising, given that the U.S. government issues the reports. Nevertheless, the State Department Web site is interesting because it represents the perspective of powerful international actors. It provides a clear illustration of the paradox of the international system: Nation-states are to act independently while simultaneously aspiring to identical goals and ultimately doing all the same things.

The paradox of taking action that is independent but identical exists for both the policymaking process and the content of policies. The international system and the United States concur that all countries should have representative democracies. Indeed, nation-states, when represented in the U.N. General Assembly and other international arenas, are imagined to be constitutive of their national populations. This is an important justification for sovereign autonomy (see Onuf 1995).[1]

At the same time, the international community wants all countries to aspire to the same goals (e.g., reduce pollution, allow women to work outside the home, end child labor). But there is a contradiction in promoting democracy locally while at the same demanding conformity to international norms. It suggests that democracy is a good thing in the developing world if—and only if—it leads to a promotion of values cherished by Westerners. It denies the possibility that there could be a popularly elected leader who does not share the values of the West.

In fact, two competing conceptions—emphasizing either local or international influence on states—suggest very different patterns of lawmaking. Of course, both conceptions hold some truth and have some historical justification (Ruggie 1993). Further, the accuracy of either conception is likely to vary across countries and issues (Thomas and Meyer 1984). Sharon Preves and I (2000) emphasized the dichotomy in a recent article to highlight what we saw as the problematic neglect of the international conception. I have updated our earlier analysis and highlight important new developments throughout this chapter.

Generally speaking, if laws are *local* creations, then every nation-state will comprise fairly unique local identities and unique laws will emerge from each local culture and power structure. According to this perspective, by thoroughly understanding local interests and power relationships, a person can explain why laws were adopted and how various local groups are likely to respond to them. If, on the other hand, *international culture* is the driving force behind national laws, then each nation-state will build its identity around commonly held universal ideals. Under the latter scenario, laws will diffuse more rapidly and look more similar than under the former scenario. The meaning of the law for various local groups under the international conception will be very different than under the local conception of control.

If nation-states are primarily influenced by local societies, they will adopt relatively unique approaches to FGC. Anti-FGC laws and policies should be least common in countries where rates of FGC exceed 50 percent of the female population because such laws will be opposed by a majority of individuals in those countries. The timing of these policies would correspond to important local events such as—in the West—increasing immigration from practicing cultures. The language of anti-FGC laws would reflect the unique character of each local culture. Finally, local activists, under such a scenario, would target national governments to create anti-FGC policies.

In contrast, if international normative pressure is more influential than local pressure, then very different outcomes should ensue. Anti-FGC laws would be most common in countries with high rates of FGC because the international community would target those countries. The laws would be passed at similar times in different countries, and their passage would coincide with international events. The language of the laws would follow a common script. And local activists would lobby international actors to create anti-FGC policies. These competing conceptions and their empirical implications are the focus of this chapter. To arbitrate between these scenarios, I trace the international history of national laws and policies opposing FGC.

A preliminary question is whether and to what extent "informal"—that is, nonlegal—anti-FGC policies represent support for the international norm against FGC. Formal laws suggest a more coordinated opposition to FGC. For example, in a number of countries, such as Kenya and Egypt, legislation was proposed and failed. In other countries, such as Tanzania, formal legislation was passed. This suggests that opposition to FGC is stronger in Tanzania than in Egypt and Kenya. The formality of a policy is relevant as one possible indicator of the degree of conformity to international ideas. Nevertheless, a government's stated position on FGC is also important. When stated opposition to FGC is considered, nearly every country where FGC occurs falls into line with the international norm.

Local Majority Sentiments

If nations are primarily interested in representing local culture, then those countries in which a majority of the families practice FGC are the least likely to take legal action to eradicate the practice. In contrast, if nations are reacting to an international audience, then these countries will be the most likely to adopt such laws. There are fourteen countries where a majority of the families practice FGC: Burkina Faso, Chad, Côte D'Ivoire, Djibouti, Egypt, Eritrea, Ethiopia, Gambia, Guinea, Mali, Nigeria, Sierra Leone, Somalia, and Sudan.[2] Three of these countries—Chad, Egypt, and Sierra Leone—have very vocal opponents to eradication efforts (U.S. Department of State 2000). Although this suggests local citizen support for or dissensus over FGC, in every one of these countries, if a government exists, it is attempting to eradicate the practice (U.S. Department of State 1998). Table 5.1 provides a brief description of the particular national policies. As the table shows, actions range from education campaigns to the passage of criminal laws.

In fact, the Egyptian actions against FGC in some ways exemplify the typical outcome in the fourteen countries where a majority of women are circumcised.[3] In each of the countries, if a government exists, it has adopted a formal eradication policy. It is also significant that the Egyptian state sponsored a health ministry decree when the parliament refused to pass a law banning FGC. As table 5.1 shows, the adoption of bureaucratic policies that circumvent the decisions of popularly elected bodies is not uncommon.

The point is that, because *all* of the African governments reached the same conclusion in a very short period of time, when FGC became counternormative internationally, anti-FGC policies were driven by the international norm: the national processes, although unique, were not independent.

Even in the three countries where there is strong opposition to eliminating FGC—Sierra Leone, Chad, and Egypt—the governments do not openly endorse the practice. In Sierra Leone, years of civil war have undermined state stability, so there is no formal state policy on FGC. However, in 1997, the leader of one of the warring factions, Johnny Paul Koroma, stated that he supported FGC and that if he took control of the country, FGC would remain legal (U.S. Department of State 1997). Recently, FGC and male circumcision (as well as other forms of physical torture) have been imposed as punishment on prisoners of war in the country. There is debate about the extent to which FGC is forced on young women, but at least one woman was abducted and forced to undergo FGC in 1996.

Eighty to ninety percent of women in Sierra Leone are circumcised (U.S. Department of State 2000). FGC is a coming-of-age ritual seen as comparable to male circumcision there (Ahmadu 2000). Initiates are circumcised in cohorts, and FGC signals entry into a powerful secret society of women. Traditionally, women and men had distinct roles but were equally powerful among Sierra Leone's Kono ethnic group. Further, Kono culture was in part matriarchal and female chastity was not centrally important. Support for FGC may remain strong in Sierra

Table 5.1 National Anti-FGC Policies

Country	Percent of Women Circumcised	Year Policies Initiated	Anti-FGC Legislation, Regulation, or Bureaucratic Action
Australia	Negligible	1993	Child abuse law
Austria	Negligible		Application of existing laws
Belgium	Negligible		Application of existing laws
Benin	5–50%		Government cooperation with NGOs; action plan; no formal law
Burkina Faso	60–70%	1996	Penal Code prohibition; education plan; sensitization campaign
Cameroon	Rare		Sponsorship of international workshop on eradicating FGC; government outspoken in opposition to practice, but no formal law
Canada	Negligible	1993	Amendment to existing Criminal Code & Youth Offenders Act
Central African Republic	43%	1996	Ordinance; awareness campaign
Chad	60%	1995	Law adopted by transitional government and signed by president makes FGC theoretically prosecutable as a form of assault. There are active and sustained public education campaigns, but there is strong opposition to eradication.
Côte d'Ivoire	As high as 60%	1998	Law Concerning Crimes against Women; NGO campaigns
Djibouti	90–98%	1995	Penal Code prohibition; no convictions thus far; UNFD campaign
Egypt	97%	1996	Health ministry decree; NGO and government education campaigns; enforcement of decree, but strong opposition to eradication
Eritrea	95%		The government discourages FGC through education programs, but there is no formal law.
Ethiopia	73–90%	1994	The constitution prohibits harmful traditional practices.
France	Negligible	1982	Assault law applied to FGC
Gambia	60–90%		Health education; government support for eradication; no formal law
Ghana	15–30%	1994	National criminal law; five arrests in 1998; local NGO and government education campaigns
Guinea	50–90%		Application of existing laws

Table 5.1 Continued

Country	Percent of Women Circumcised	Year Policies Initiated	Anti-FGC Legislation, Regulation, or Bureaucratic Action
Guinea-Bissau	50%		Education campaign; coordination with international NGOs; efforts suspended after outbreak of fighting in June 1998 resumed in February 1999; no formal law
Kenya	38%	2001	FGC banned by presidential decree
Liberia	As high as 50% in rural areas		FGC was undermined by disruption of villages during civil war, but there is no formal law.
Mali	94%		Application of existing laws
Mauritania	25%		Hospital ban; education campaign; no formal law
Niger	20%		Government firmly committed to eradication; cooperation with UNICEF; no formal law
Nigeria	60%	1999	Some state laws; no federal law
Senegal	5–20%	1999	National ban
Sierra Leone	80–90%		Faction likely to assume power opposes the eradication of FGC; secret societies have circumcised women against their will, and there is no formal law.
Somalia	98%	1999	Some local bans; 1991 law passed by former administration no longer enforced
Sudan	90% of women in the north	1991	Health law (no criminal law); NGO/government education campaigns
Sweden	Negligible	1982	National ban
Switzerland	Negligible	1983	National ban
Tanzania	18%	1998	National ban
The Netherlands	Negligible		Application of child abuse law
Togo	12%	1998	National ban, but no prosecutions; seminars
Uganda	5%		UNFPA education program, supported by the government, has reduced the incidence by one-third, but there is no formal law.
U.K.	Negligible	1985	National ban
United States	Negligible	1991	Local bans beginning in 1991; national ban 1996

Table 5.1 Continued

Note: IGO = international governmental organization; NGO = nongovernmental organization; UNFD = Union of Djiboutian Women; UNFPA = U.N. Family Planning Association.

Sources: These data are taken from several sources (Bashir 1996; James 1994; Smith 1995; U.S. Department of State 1996 through 2000; Rahman and Toubia 2000). Much of this information comes from State Department reports, which are based on country reports from embassies in the local countries. Naturally, the emphasis on particular types of action varies from country to country. We spoke with the State Department official who constructs the FGC portion of the reports and were impressed by her meticulous attention to detail and her sensitivity to the different biases surrounding the issue.

Leone not only because of the lack of a stable government but also because many of the Western characterizations of FGC (that FGC is a tool of patriarchy, for instance) do not describe the practice well there.

In Chad, the government has demonstrated its commitment to eradicating FGC. In 2000, the Chad Council of Ministers passed a law to criminalize FGC, but the National Assembly had still not taken action on the law at the time of this writing. It is estimated that 60 percent of women in Chad are circumcised. Although all types of FGC are practiced in the country, clitoridectomy is the most common. As in Sierra Leone, FGC in Chad typically marks the passage into puberty. However, Leonard (2000) found that young girls in Myabé were seeking FGC as a fashion statement. A number of these girls, whose mothers were not circumcised, were undergoing FGC without their parents' consent or even against their parents' wishes.

The situation in Egypt was explained in detail in chapter 1. In that country, the government, under pressure from the international community, has taken steps to eradicate FGC. The practice has considerable local support in the country, however, and the Egyptian parliament has been unable to pass legislation against FGC. The fact that all countries with an active government currently have an anti-FGC policy among the fourteen where FGC is a majority tradition suggests that local culture is not particularly influential in motivating legal action within this group of nations. This is true despite the prediction several years ago that African governments could not "afford" to listen to international edicts against FGC (Weinstein 1983, 175).

In other African states, where FGC is practiced by less than a majority of women, governments are currently taking clear public stands against the practice.[4] Among the countries in which FGC is *not* practiced by a majority of the families, there are eleven countries where FGC occurs at a measurable rate (Benin, Central African Republic, Ghana, Guinea-Bissau, Kenya, Liberia, Mauritania, Niger, Senegal, Tanzania, and Togo) and two in which FGC is rare (Cameroon and Uganda). The consistent anti-FGC position of these states is not surprising from either a local or an international perspective. It makes sense that FGC is a contested issue in these countries: competing intranational groups could be vying to define national culture, with the edge going to the majorities. It also seems empirically likely that local majority opinion and international pressure will coincide in these countries. In the West, levels of FGC are negligible. Passing laws seems somewhat odd because of the extremely low numbers involved. On the other hand, moral opposition to the practice has almost no counterweight in these countries. In other words, there are no vocal supporters of FGC in Western countries. I discuss this more in the next section.

Empirically, the pattern of policy adoption supports the importance of international influence. Local rates of FGC are *not* a good predictor of whether a country has taken steps to eradicate FGC. In fact, the overwhelming majority of countries in which most women have been circumcised nevertheless formally forbid the practice. A better predictor of *inaction* is structural: countries with no active government are the only countries in which FGC is common that have failed to undertake some kind of eradication effort. A better predictor of *action* for these countries seems to be their peripheral location in the international system.

Events Prompting National Female Genital Cutting Policies

If nation-states are attuned primarily to local interests, local events should be most influential in the timing of anti-FGC policies. Despite a century of opposition to the practice, nation-states generally did not pass anti-FGC legislation until a structured international opposition was in place (table 5.1). Overall, then, recent legislation coincides with the emergence of opposition to FGC at the international level. Here, I consider that trend in more detail.

One of the first surprising findings for those who take a local perspective on national policymaking is that anti-FGC laws are quite common in Organization for Economic Cooperation and Development countries, where FGC is practically nonexistent. A common assumption is that laws in Western countries were passed in response to a large influx of immigrants from practicing cultures. But the "responding to massive immigration" argument does not necessarily hold when examining rates of immigration from countries with high rates of FGC. Take, for example, the United States, which passed a federal anti-FGC law in 1996. Although rates of migration to the United States steadily increased between 1955 and 1995,[5] African immigration accounted for only a small proportion of this populace shift. In fact, between 1985 and 1995, immigration from countries where FGC is practiced remained well under 4 percent of total immigration (U.S. Department of Justice 1995). Among this small number of immigrants, the percentage of those likely to have the procedure was even smaller because most immigrants are male and perhaps have more of a Western orientation than those who do not emigrate.

The legislative history suggests that the U.S. anti-FGC law did not pass sooner precisely because legislators thought the practice too infrequent to justify congressional action. In support of the legislation, its co-sponsor, Congresswoman Patricia Schroeder, stated, "Over 100 million girls and women in the world have undergone some form of [FGC], and I have received anecdotal reports that it is happening here" (Congressional Record 1995a). Later the congresswoman suggested, "The problem in this Congress seems to be that Members still do not believe that such a brutal procedure happens in this country" (Congressional Record 1995b). In addition, prior to the passage of the federal law in 1996, the vast majority of U.S. states had fewer than 4 African refugees per 10,000 in the population, and in raw terms, most states had fewer than 1,000 refugees total from practicing cultures (U.S. Department of Justice 1995). Although the number of immigrants from practicing cultures increased somewhat in the late 1990s, no study documents any systematic occurrence of FGC in the United States.

It was only when a woman from Togo requested asylum in the United States to avoid FGC that the United States acted to ban the practice (Congressional Record 1995c). At that point, the legislative history makes references to the anti-FGC laws of "many nations," including the U.K. and Sudan, and the supportive position of the World Health Organization, UNICEF, and other international human rights groups (Congressional Record 1995b). Based on the arguments of the Immigration and Naturalization Service, the United States seemed at least as interested in limiting the number of future refugees as actually stopping FGC. In addition, setting the moral high ground in the international community and avoiding the embarrassment connected with the imprisonment of the asylum seeker also appear to have been dominant concerns.

Levels of FGC appear not to have been a prime motivating factor for legislative action at the state level in the United States either. In all U.S. states, the number of refugees from nations where FGC is practiced was quite small prior to 1996. The highest number of refugees, relative to the population of the state, was in South Dakota. There, refugees from Ethiopia, Liberia, Somalia, and Sudan numbered 12 for every 10,000 in the population. Still, South Dakota did not legally ban FGC. Preceding the federal ban, California, Delaware, Illinois, Michigan, Minnesota, North Dakota, Rhode Island, Tennessee, and Wisconsin outlawed FGC between 1994 and 1996 (see Dugger 1996; Coleman 1998). In 1996, these states ranked tenth, thirty-seventh, twenty-first, thirtieth, seventh, eighth, seventeenth, fifteenth, and thirty-third, respectively, in terms of the number of African refugees per 10,000 people (U.S. Department of Justice 1995).

Prior to the passage of the Michigan legislation, reporters for the *Detroit News* attempted unsuccessfully to uncover any cases of FGC in the city (McCann and Angell 1993). California legislation was based in part on reports that five women had required deinfibulation prior to childbirth in San Jose, a very small number considering the size of the city. The legislative history for the California ban on FGC refers to anti-FGC legislation in Sweden, the U.K., France, the Netherlands, and Belgium as well as mentioning international organizations, treaties, and conferences that oppose the practice (California State

Senate 1997). The Minnesota legislation followed the reporting of one case of FGC (Anderson 1994). Given the small number of immigrants and the even smaller number of reported incidents of FGC, actual rates of immigration do not seem to be a precipitating factor in the passage of U.S. state anti-FGC legislation.

When the U.S. banned FGC, there were no formal estimates of how many girls were at risk of FGC. The U.S. legislation approved funding for a study to determine this number. After conducting the study, the Centers for Disease Control estimated that there were 48,000 girls whose parents claimed ancestry from cultures where FGC is practiced (Jones et al. 1997, 372). Of course, that includes many nonrefugee families. Counting actual refugees from practicing cultures who arrived in the United States after 1986 would result in a much lower estimate.

Continuing the analysis, if citizen interests were driving policies, we would expect the timing of anti-FGC policies to coincide with specific intranational disputes. Viewed as a group, these policies would occur sporadically. If, alternatively, international forces had a greater effect on anti-FGC policies, many national policies would be adopted within a short period of time as the international community brought its resources to bear against FGC. Based on this reasoning, the facts again support the importance of international influence. Nearly all the policies were adopted after international organizing was established—specifically, the Copenhagen conference in 1980. At that point, an interesting pattern began to develop. National laws began to occur in clusters, with the West acting first. France, Sweden, Switzerland, and the U.K. were the forerunners in the passage of anti-FGC legislation or the explicit application of existing legislation to the practice (table 5.1). When African nations did not immediately respond in kind, international instruments became increasingly specific in their opposition to FGC. In 1996, the United States passed the legislation that linked foreign aid to anti-FGC policies. Although a number of African countries had adopted policies or passed legislation prior to the U.S. legislation, complete uniformity in national policies (with the previously noted exception of Sierra Leone) was achieved after the U.S. legislation.

The impact of the U.S. legislation indicates that the adoption of uniform policies is often not entirely voluntary among nation-states. Hegemonic definitions of proper national action may spread through coercive action. Nevertheless, even under a scenario of direct pressure—in fact, especially under a scenario of direct pressure—the importance of the international community in understanding national legal action is critical. Overall, having national legal action follow international organizing and having the West act first, followed by practicing cultures, suggests an international pattern of activity.

Wording and Isomorphism

Next, let us consider the language of national laws. In this regard, if nation-states were constitutive of their local citizenry, laws would be tailored to the specific situations of the countries that pass them. Colonial laws early in the century did indeed have this quality. So, for example, a 1946 law in Sudan banned only one type of FGC, infibulation:

> Unlawful circumcision:
> 1. Section 284 A(I). Whoever voluntarily causes hurt to the external genital organs of a women is said, save as hereinafter excepted, to commit unlawful circumcision.
> Exceptions: It is not an offense against this section merely to remove the free and projecting part of the clitoris. (El Dareer 1982, 95)

Likewise, the 1959 Egyptian Health Decree specifically incorporated the local context:

> Although Islamic Jurists, basing their arguments on verified *ahadith* have differed on whether *Khafd* is a duty, a *sunna,* or *makrama,* yet they have all agreed that it is an Islamic ritual and that Sharia law forbids total clitoridectomy. Therefore, the committee sees the necessity to proceed with the *Khafd* operation in the following order: (1) it is absolutely forbidden for other than doctors to perform the operation, (2) for those who want circumcision, the operation should be partial and not total clitoridectomy. (Assaad 1980, 5)

This suggests that, at mid-century, local interests were active in tailoring legislation to address their own specific concerns.

When external forces are important, we would expect to see little variation or tailoring among national laws. Rather, national laws will follow a particular script that completely bans FGC. Alternate scripts medicalizing the procedure or limiting the type of procedure (e.g., banning only infibulation) will be discouraged by the international community. Modern laws have all these features. By the 1990s, the international community was willing to accept only laws mandating complete eradication of the practice. Consequently, today's anti-FGC laws do not medicalize the procedure and do not distinguish among the different types of FGC: they simply ban all forms of the practice. They differ only in their reach: some ban FGC for only persons under 18 (e.g., the U.S. law); others specify that consent is not a defense (e.g., the Canada law) (Rahman and Toubia 2000). Thus, the substance of the laws is the same; only the breadth of their applicability varies.

The U.S. federal ban provides a specific example of the international anti-FGC script. The law is modeled explicitly after the U.K.'s 1985 federal ban on FGC (Bashir 1996). The explicit language in the 1985 British ban reads that under this act it is an offense to "excise, infibulate, or otherwise mutilate the whole or any part of the labia majora or labia minora or clitoris of another person" (Black and Debelle 1995, 3). The consequence for such action includes "a fine or imprisonment for up to five years, or both" (Black and Debelle 1995, 3). In the U.S. language, "Whoever knowingly circumcises, *excises, or infibulates the whole or any part of the labia majora or labia minora or clitoris of another person* who has not attained the age of 18 years shall be *fined under this title or imprisoned not more than 5 years, or both*" (Congressional Record 1996, similar language is italicized). The similarity of this legislative language illustrates that the United States looked to the U.K. statute in devising the statutory wording. Similarly, in Australia, the legislative language banning FGC was explicitly modeled off of Canadian legislation (Ierodiaconou 1995, footnote 62). The importance of external forces is evidenced by marked similarities that characterize many of the laws passed both in the West and in African nations. The rhetoric surrounding the issue clearly treated national legal action as part of an international project. For example, laws banning the

practice were frequently cited in the context of "international statements against FGC" (see Black and Debelle 1995; Ierodiaconou 1995;
Hughes 1995).

Central Actors

Finally, the extent to which activists viewed national actors as the insti-
gators of change is an indicator of the relative importance of national
influences. If nation-states were relatively autonomous local units,
then the initial efforts to eradicate FGC would be directed against national governments. If nation-states were actors who simply play by
the rules of the international community, then efforts would be directed toward the international community. In fact, the pattern of
activity shows that Western feminists and nongovernmental organizations (NGOs) interested in the issue tended to bypass local governments and appeal directly to citizens or directly to international
organizations to take action. In the last chapter, I discussed the actions of international organizations. I will only briefly revisit some of
those actions here. In the mid-1970s, local African NGOs directed
their attention specifically to African citizens (in local radio shows and
seminars), but by the late 1970s, NGOs began to direct their attention to international organizations. For example, they sent detailed
information to the secretary-general of the United Nations. Further,
in looking at the national policies developed to eradicate FGC (see
table 5.1), one sees many partnerships between NGOs, international
governmental organizations, and nation-states.

An important pattern emerges in relations between local areas and
the international community. Keck and Sikkink (1998) describe a
"boomerang effect" of international action: individuals confront national governments, but if their efforts are thwarted at the national
level, they then turn to the international community to apply pressure. (This is called a boomerang effect because pressure from below
"comes back" to the state in the form of pressure from above.) The
pattern of national policymaking for FGC is generally consistent with
Keck and Sikkink's analysis but suggests that some subtle modifications are needed. First, with respect to certain issues such as FGC, in
many countries, local actors may not even attempt action at the na-

tional level. If actors believe efficacious outcomes are unlikely, they may bypass national governments altogether and head directly for the international system. More importantly, this analysis addresses *why* local pressure often does not effect national change: actors in the international system rather than local citizens are often the constituents to which nation-states appeal. There certainly were local movements against FGC in African countries; it would be absurd to suggest otherwise. However, it may be true that movements were effective not because of their standing within local power structures but because they tapped into and supported a discourse opposed to FGC at the international level.

This chapter has shown that the policies of separate nation-states are not always the outcome of local political processes. The occurrence of anti-FGC policies in countries where many individuals support the practice, the timing and character of national legal action directed against FGC, and the uniformity of political action all lend weight to the importance of international pressure in the adoption of anti-FGC policies. Policies against FGC have not varied much based on local mobilization and political organization. This implies that the ruling elites of countries have been playing to a larger global community as much as to a local audience. The research discussed here suggests that for some questions, focusing on only local actors can lead to an incomplete, even spurious, explanation for phenomena. Rather than an analysis that privileges either the international or the local, a careful multilevel analysis that considers the sources of identity construction—not only for individuals but also for organizations and states—seems essential.

These findings have several implications for international actors and the international system as well. First, the contradiction among institutions at the international level can put a check on the progression of any particular ideal (cf. Friedland and Alford 1991). Specifically, in the contest between democratic representation and universal human rights in the FGC realm, the human rights ideal dominates (see also Soysal 1994; Obiora 1997). Nation-states adopt laws that prohibit the practice even when the laws do not reflect their local constituencies. Nevertheless, the institution of representative democracy continues to have an important effect on the process. This is evident in the deference that international governmental organizations give to the sovereign authority of nation-states. These organizations use primarily assimilative strategies, including African nations in the policymaking process, having Western countries "model" appropriate national action, and promoting local anti-FGC mobilization within African countries. Respect for sovereign autonomy influences international actors to adopt less intrusive assimilative reform policies rather than more directly instrumental, coercive policies. In contrast, actors in the international system who exist apart from the sovereignty system (NGOs, the media, etc.) or who represent hegemonic authority (the United States, France, etc.) may be less deferential to sovereign authority. This suggests that there are many possibilities for social development at the point where institutions contradict.

Second, this research demonstrates a conception of power that contrasts with other recent conceptions (see, e.g., Silbey 1997, 227–28)—one that recognizes the empowering possibilities of the global narrative. Power and exploitation exist on many levels in the world. Daly (1978) linked FGC to patriarchal family, religion, and political structures that exploit women. At the same time, Obiora (1997; see also Gunning 1990–91) links Western pressures regarding FGC to postcolonial imperialism. Although Western pressure forced nation-states where FGC occurs to adopt anti-FGC policies, many would characterize international mobilization against FGC as *empowering* local women who did not want to undergo the practice. Thus, whether the international system stripped away power or provided power is an open question. In fact, it appears to have done both. An institutional analysis raises a new perspective on power in the international system.

Recapping the similarities in national action, international pressure (or at least avoiding international embarrassment) uniformly influenced the adoption of national policies—often laws. In addition, all nations' actions tended to be directed largely to an international audience. Further, activists from different countries used similar rhetoric that invoked the institutions carried by the international system: women's rights as human rights, the unfairness of patriarchy, and the need to correct for the implicit lack of free will among third-world women.

Despite these similarities, variation did exist. Western countries were generally the first to adopt anti-FGC legislation despite the small number of cases involved within their borders. Also, because of the small number of cases of FGC in these countries, international pressure to pass laws was dramatically lower than on some African countries. Among Western countries, former colonial powers were well represented in the group that passed laws: Belgium, France, the Netherlands, the U.K., and the United States. Of the other Western countries, two (Australia and Canada) have strong historical ties to the U.K. The political organization of these countries may also have played a role (cf. Boyle 1998). A full accounting of variation in international participation among Western powers is beyond the scope of this text, but it does seem that those with more historical links to the international system were overrepresented among the trendsetters.

Countries on the "periphery" of the international system where FGC does not occur appear not to be involved in the mobilization against the practice. These countries may have in fact adopted policies against FGC that simply have not been discussed in the international literature, but a more likely scenario is that they are not actively involved in the prohibition efforts. Explaining inaction is always difficult. These countries may lack the resources to monitor all international issues, they may have less "moral capital" than other countries to lead campaigns for change, they may oppose the international efforts, or they may be busy dealing with "culture clashes" of their own. These countries' absence from the debates may be an indicator of how quickly anti-FGC sentiment became institutionalized in the international system. It is assumed that people do not circumcise their daughters in modern countries and that only countries with a history of FGC need to distance themselves from the practice. On the other hand, the absence of most peripheral countries may also bring into question the true universality of international efforts.

A further key difference involves the character of national laws. Western countries have tended to pass formal laws, while African countries have been more likely to establish policy bureaucratically, through presidential or health minister decrees. By avoiding formal legislation, African countries have been better able to decouple local sentiment from their legal actions. This variation suggests that local concerns matter more in determining the *formality* of legal action to eradicate FGC than in the actual *adoption* of that policy goal. If local sentiment has opposed eradication, legal action has been less formal than if local sentiment has supported eradication. These differences are analyzed in more depth in the following chapter.

SIX

Variation in the Meanings of National Policies

FGM was pictured as a tradition that constitutes part of . . . [Egypt's] code of ethics and morals, as opposed to the ethics and morals being "imposed" by the West. Thereby a battle was launched between two stereotypes, neither of which exists in reality so much as in theory and imagination.
— *Aida Seif El Dawla, "The Political and Legal Struggle over Female Genital Mutilation in Egypt," 1999*

Recent international activism attacking FGC has been very successful in getting countries to adopt policies against the practice. In some ways, then, legislating against FGC seems like a typical diffusion story: a few key countries adopt a policy, and other countries follow suit. As demonstrated in the last two chapters, international organizations played an important role in these developments.

Although this is an important insight, there is more to the story. In focusing on global diffusion, neoinstitutional theory tends to gloss over variations in national policies. In part, this tendency is due to the use of statistical methods that conceptualize policy implementation as a binary phenomenon—either a country has a policy or it does not. But by simply counting the presence or absence of a policy, the theory cannot capture differences in (1) local conflicts surrounding reforms, (2) the processes of policy adoption, and (3) the interaction of global and local politics. In fact, anti-FGC policies do exemplify the typical diffusion pattern, but they also bring new aspects of diffusion to the fore.

Theorizing Cross-National Variation in Policies

In general, countries in the periphery of the world system appear to have less ability to opt out of international reform (cf. DiMaggio and Powell 1983). For example, in their analysis of international arbitration, Dezalay and Garth (1996) asked why Southern nations participated in the international arbitration system, despite its Western bias. The answer was that Southern nations had no other options; international arbitration was the only legitimate outlet when business conflicts emerged. Likewise, Finnemore (1996) found that the least developed countries were often the most likely to adopt national science ministries, even though they had the least to gain from such bureaucracies. The general theme of these examples is that peripheral nations, because they rely on core nations for much of their resources, are under pressure to mimic core nations.[1]

The case of FGC illustrates the idea that power is not the only important factor driving variation in national policymaking. The "functionality" or local relevance of policies promoted by the international system is also likely to affect how policies are adopted and perceived by local individuals. Some neoinstitutionalists have suggested that functionality can actually have a negative effect on diffusion because functional policies are more concrete, forcing more explicit individual acquiescence (Boyle and Meyer 1998). In general, the role of functionality is not well understood.

Functionality and power combine to influence the level of contestation generated by reform efforts, as illustrated by countries' responses to international pressure. This occurs as follows: Contestation is likely when the reform serves a concrete function locally—that is, when it is relevant to local individuals. For example, anti-FGC reforms should meet with more opposition in Mali than in Sweden because the policies have more direct relevance in Mali, where it is estimated that 94 percent of women are circumcised.

Relevance, then, is a necessary condition for contestation. But by itself it may not be sufficient to generate high levels of contestation. Among countries where a policy has local relevance, a nation's standing in the international system will also be critically important. Contestation, when it occurs, should be greater in countries with more leverage in the international system. Nations with more leverage have more ability to actually shape rather than simply receive policy edicts. Individuals in these nations are likely to have more resources on average, which provides more ability to mobilize opposition to international norms. For instance, because Egypt has more leverage in the international system than Tanzania does, it will be more able to opt out of global reforms. At the same time, because it is a relatively powerful country, Egypt is also likely to experience greater international media coverage than Tanzania (see chapter 4). The consequences of power will interact to create higher levels of contestation in Egypt. In sum, holding policy relevance constant, nations with more resources will tend to generate more contestation over policies.

When considering national uniqueness in the process of banning FGC, other issues also arise. Does more contestation result in less public input into the policymaking process? In countries with high levels of opposition, state leaders may attempt to avoid negative publicity by quietly and informally adopting policies. Representative bodies may be avoided. If a policy's content risks resurrecting old national political conflicts, do state leaders emphasize the perspective of "neutral" international actors? Finally, are policies adopted pursuant to a process of international diffusion more "extranationally" directed in the West than in the periphery? These issues are mentioned from time to time throughout this chapter.

Fortunata Songora, Gail Foss, and I (2001) conducted case studies of anti-FGC policies in Egypt, Tanzania, and the United States to explore these theoretical ideas. I relate much of the findings from that analysis here. The primary common element across the three countries is that all acquiesced to the international norm against FGC by adopting national anti-FGC policies. Both Egypt and the United States passed laws against FGC in 1996. Tanzania began prosecuting cases of FGC under its criminal code in 1995 and adopted specific anti-FGC legislation in 1998. Growing international sentiment aimed at eradicating the practice of FGC influenced action in all of the countries.

There are also some obvious differences between the three countries. The United States is wealthier and has more leverage than any other country in the international system. Egypt, with its oil reserves, American military base, and historical leadership role among Islamic countries, is a significant but peripheral international player. Tanzania is a poor country hit hard by an AIDS crisis. Tanzania's external debt is $7.6 billion—94.3 percent of the country's total gross national product (World Bank 2000). The country uses millions of dollars of its revenues each year to service its debts. Of the three countries, Tanzania has the least pull in the international community.

Besides international standing, another distinguishing factor is the relationship between religion and politics. The United States is predominantly Christian, but courts and other state-run institutions are secular. Tanzania includes a mix of Christians, Muslims, and followers of indigenous religions. As in the United States, the government is secular. Recently, religious differences have fueled political tension in Tanzania. Egypt is predominantly Muslim and has a semisecular state (see Brown 1995). Islam is the official state religion. Importantly, Egypt is home to Al-Azhar University, the oldest and most prestigious institution of higher education in the Islamic world. Because of the tremendous respect accorded the University, Egyptian administrations have maintained close ties to the institution. Several high-profile religious leaders at Al-Azhar University figured prominently in the debate over FGC in the 1990s.

Finally, the countries differ in the prevalence of FGC. FGC is rare in the United States. With the exception of binary sex surgeries, the practice is believed to occur solely among recent groups of immigrants. In Tanzania, a sizable minority of families practice FGC. An estimated 18 percent of women in the country are circumcised (U.S. Department of State 2000). The practice occurs in 20 of 130 ethnic groups in Tanzania and among Somali immigrants to the country (Center for Reproductive Law and Policy and International Federation of Women Lawyers 1997). In Tanzania, the cutting is performed by a *ngariba* ("keeper of the tradition") or traditional birth attendant, or by a trained doctor or midwife (Nkoma-Wamunza et al. 1998; Mabala and Kamazima 1995). There have been a number of reported deaths from FGC in Tanzania. For example, in the Tarime district, out of the estimated 5,000 circumcisions performed each year, about 20 girls die as a result of the procedure (Temba 1997; Lukaya 1997). Egypt has the highest rates of FGC. In Egypt, 97 percent of married women have been circumcised, and, until very recently, 88 percent of women in the country either favored the continuation of the practice (82 percent) or had no opinion about its continuation (6 percent) (Carr 1997).

Policies in African Countries

Unlike in the West, where FGC has been a political issue only recently, some African countries have debated about FGC for decades. FGC is on the front line of a "culture" war between "traditionalists" and "modernists" (Griswold 1994, 111–12).

In terms of their function, FGC policies in Egypt are relevant to nearly all local individuals because the rate of FGC is very high there. In terms of international standing, Egypt is moderately powerful. Egypt is very dependent on the West for resources (e.g., revenues from tourism). On the other hand, Egypt's unique position in the Middle East makes it one of the most powerful countries in Africa. The conflict between appealing to Western investors and demonstrating a commitment to traditional Islam has been inherited by the current Egyptian administration of Hosni Mubarak and frames the Egyptian political battles over FGC (Moustafa 2000). Based on this combination of functionality and a relatively high level of international influence, Egypt's anti-FGC policies should be more contested than those of the United States and Tanzania.

There has been a small but active anti-FGC contingent in Egypt since the 1920s (Dillon 2000). In the 1950s—around the time Egypt gained its independence—local anti-FGC activists achieved some success. The first independent Egyptian administration, under Gamal Abdul Nasser, took mild action against FGC (Metz 1990). The health minister at the time (about 1959) issued a decree forbidding infibulation in public hospitals but allowing clitoridectomies at the request of parents (Assaad 1980; Dillon 2000). This partial ban on FGC was never publicized or enforced under Nasser or under the subsequent administration of Anwar Sadat (Assaad 1980). The decree may have been successful in moving Egyptians toward a milder form of FGC, but it did not diminish the number of women undergoing the procedure.

To recap events from the last decade, when international pressure to eradicate FGC mounted, Egyptian authorities were initially able to evade it. The government maintained that the practice was dying out. After CNN aired an Egyptian girl's circumcision in 1994, this position became less tenable. Nevertheless, Egypt did not respond with rote conformity to international pressure. As described in the introduction, Egypt's anti-FGC stance was highly contested. Although the government indicated its interest in passing legislation to make FGC illegal,[2] this attempt was unsuccessful. A prominent sheikh supported the practice publicly. Formal legislation was further impeded when a task force formed by the health minister denounced the idea of criminalizing FGC (Dillon 2000). Instead, the national health minister reissued the once-forgotten 1959 ban on the practice in state hospitals and clinics. As a result of pressure from powerful Muslim leaders, this ban was eventually rescinded.

In 1996, the United States passed legislation that linked foreign aid to anti-FGC policies. In addition, Macro International released its findings that 97 percent of married Egyptian women had been circumcised. One researcher involved in the administration of the survey indicated that "the Egyptians thought this was a dying custom and . . . this was much, much higher than they had expected" (Lancaster 1996, A14). Faced with nearly irrefutable evidence that FGC was persisting, the health minister reversed his position yet again and forbade the performance of FGC in any government medical facility.

Although eventually succumbing to international pressure, the Egyptian state and anti-FGC activists in Egypt have clearly attempted to distance themselves from international actors. Seham Abd el Salam is an Egyptian woman who runs anti-FGC seminars. A recurring theme she hears from fellow Egyptians is that attempts to eradicate FGC are part of a Western conspiracy to undermine Egyptian culture (Dillon 2000). Likewise, the refusal of the health minister's task force to recommend legislation appears to be an indication of local independence and resistance. Local Egyptian feminist organizations are also harshly critical of the U.S. threat to cut off financial aid: "This . . . give[s] credibility to what Egyptian people are being told by fundamentalist institutions and individuals—that circumcision is part of their identity, which they should defend against a Western world that seeks to dominate them" (Seif El Dawla 1999, 134). This resistance reflects Egypt's ability to operate somewhat independently of international pressure. Such resistance would have been more difficult in a country with less leverage in the international system, as illustrated by the case of Tanzania.

To successfully oppose FGC, the executive branch had to distance itself from the legislature. The legislature was unwilling to make FGC illegal, so President Mubarak devised a bureaucratic solution to the contest—a health ministry decree. The state also began prosecuting a limited number of individuals for botched circumcisions. The wife of President Mubarak, Suzanne Mubarak, now plays a personal role in making the Egyptian public aware of the dangers of FGC. All of these strategies have operated apart from local popular sentiment; indeed, they have been specifically geared toward *changing* that sentiment. The executive action and elite representations about FGC contrast strongly with actual rates of FGC in Egyptian society, illustrating how the Egyptian state distanced itself from local society.

While Egypt resisted Western intervention in its attempts to ban FGC, eradication efforts in Tanzania had a very different character. As in Egypt, the law against FGC had functional relevance in Tanzania. The practice is inseparable from the cultural identity, social values, and standards of certain peoples (United Republic of Tanzania 1999; Kijo-Bisimba et al. 1999; Nkoma-Wamunza et al. 1998). In some ethnic groups, uncircumcised women are perceived as unclean and impure (Wada 1992). Often they are described in degrading terms (Mabala and Kamazima 1995). And in some communities, uncircumcised women are forbidden from attending important social occasions, such as funerals. As these examples indicate, FGC is an important measure of status in a number of Tanzanian ethnic groups.

However, because most of its population does not practice FGC, one might have expected Tanzania to be a forerunner in anti-FGC legislation. This was not the case. Tanzania is a diverse country. For example, roughly 45 percent of the population is Muslim, 35 percent Christian, and 20 percent other religions (U.S. Central Intelligence Agency 1999). Since independence in 1961, Tanzanian presidents have included both Christians and a Muslim. Occasionally, religious tensions have led to political turmoil. The state's legitimacy is thus dependent on appearing neutral in the face of local diversity. In this context, a law against FGC would be problematic if it appeared to target particular minority groups. This may explain why Tanzania did not lead countries in opposing FGC.

At the same time, the Tanzanian state had no leverage to ignore international opposition to FGC. The country borrows internally and externally from financial institutions such as banks and corporations. Externally, it borrows from the Paris Club (developed nations), non–Paris Club members, and multilateral and bilateral corporations such as the International Monetary Fund and the World Bank (United Republic of Tanzania 1997–98). Many of these financial institutions make loans or aid conditional on countries taking certain actions. As noted above, in 1996, the United States made its funding of loans through the International Monetary Fund or World Bank contingent specifically on countries adopting anti-FGC policies. This undoubtedly caught the attention of Tanzanian officials.

The result was an enthusiastic if belated embrace of international calls to abolish FGC. Local government officials began prosecuting and imprisoning people for performing the practice in 1995. For example, in July 1995, local government officials in Dodoma fined several parents after their daughters appeared in the local health center with excessive bleeding (U.S. Department of State 1996). In 1996, local government officials imprisoned five people in an effort to prevent the practice from being performed on young girls. A formal law against the practice was passed in 1998—the Sexual Offence Special Provision Bill (Act No. 4 of 1998, Section 169). Several persons were prosecuted in that year (U.S. Department of State 1998). The bill states that FGC constitutes cruelty to children and therefore is a punishable criminal offense (Cheng and About 1999). Specifically, the bill provides: "Any person with the care, control and custody of a girl child under 18 years of age who causes that girl child to be mutilated is guilty of an offense and liable to imprisonment for a term not less than 5 years and/or to a fine. It is an offense to assault anyone or mutilate a person over the age of 18 without their consent." Note how the law uses "mutilation," a term commonly used by international actors but harshly criticized for its Western bias (see Gunning 1990–91; Obiora 1997).

In passing the law, Tanzanian authorities relied on the arguments put forward by international actors. As noted above, international organizations in the past three decades have adopted a universalistic discourse: (1) Islam does not require FGC, and the practice does not coincide with Islam; (2) promoting health is good for all; and (3) violence against women is bad for all. This is the discourse adopted by Tanzanian officials as well. For example, the director of community development in Tanzania delivered a speech stating that "FGC is against human rights and it is performed without the consent of the individuals" (United Republic of Tanzania 1999, 2–3). By placing anti-FGC mobilization within universal frames, international actors have been able to avoid claims of Western ethnocentrism. Likewise, by adopting this reasoning, the Tanzanian state has been able to attack FGC without appearing biased against any local groups.

The Tanzanian case differs from the Egyptian case in another way as well. Once it took up the issue, the Tanzanian government never formally wavered from an anti-FGC stance. The state has made no attempt to distance itself from international anti-FGC policy. On the contrary, in forming national policy, Tanzanian leaders drew heavily on international statements. For example, during a national conference on FGC in 1999, Tanzanian lawyers highlighted various international and regional statements condemning FGC (Cheng and About 1999). Nearly all studies or reports conducted in Tanzania on FGC reference the various international statements opposing the practice (United Republic of Tanzania 1999; Cheng and About 1999; Kijo-Bisimba et al. 1999; Nkoma-Wamunza et al. 1998).[3] Local newspaper articles discussing the practice and the state's response highlight the support of international actors (see, e.g., Kijo-Bisimba et al. 1999). By emphasizing the role of the international community in its reform efforts, the Tanzanian state has been able to present mobilization against FGC as a matter of global consensus—not something it thought up independently.

Although formally the Tanzanian state has steadily maintained its opposition to FGC, informally the picture is somewhat different. A recent newspaper report indicated that "parents offer cash, cattle, sheep and goats to government officials from the village to district level so that they can look the other way as the ritual goes on" (Mgamba 2001, 7). The report went on to note that an estimated 500 girls had been circumcised in the Mara region during October 2001 despite government opposition.

The importance of the West, like the importance of international organizations, is evident in Tanzania's law. The anti-FGC law is in English, despite the fact that most Tanzanians cannot speak or read English. (This is true of all Tanzanian laws.) And UNICEF (1996) drafted the anti-FGC law's implementation plan.

Overall support from the government continues despite the difficulty this support raises for some politicians. For example, in Tarime-Mara during a recent campaign, the candidates were asked if they support FGC. If their response was "no," they were not elected (Kijo-Bisimba et al. 1999). In fact, many government leaders in Tanzania are personally pro-FGC or at least afraid to take a personal stand against the practice.

Evidence is somewhat sketchy, but it appears that reform efforts are making more inroads in Tanzania than in Egypt. As of 1996, 82 percent of married Egyptian women favored the continuation of FGC (compared to the base rate of 97 percent who had been circumcised themselves). In Tanzania, Nkoma-Wamunza and others (1998) found that attitudes were changing in regions where FGC rates were high. For example, in urban Dodoma, 95 percent of both men and women wanted to see FGC abolished. The percentage of circumcised women in the region overall is 68 percent. In both Egypt and Tanzania, there is evidence that parents are requesting less extreme forms of the practice (see Kijo-Basimba et al. 1999; Mabala and Kamazima 1995). There is also some evidence that the practice is becoming medicalized in Egypt (El-Zanaty et al. 1996, 177). This may not be an option in resource-poor Tanzania.

Policies in Industrialized Countries

In the West, colonial authorities (France, the Netherlands, and Great Britain) and related countries (the United States, Australia, and Canada) were particularly active in anti-FGC efforts. The issue of FGC has little if any direct relevance to the vast majority of people in these countries. Consequently, the bans on the practice in these countries, including the United States, generated very little controversy. The

Western cases provide an interesting contrast to the cases of Tanzania and Egypt, especially in terms of the interaction between global and local forces.

France was the first Western country to prosecute cases of FGC within its borders (Winter 1994). France's first FGC trial occurred in 1979, for a circumcision that led to the death in June 1978 of a female infant. It was nearly a decade later, in 1988, when a case actually conclusively linked FGC to the French Penal Code. The code prohibits a range of violent acts against minors and attaches a punishment of ten to twenty years "if there has been mutilation, amputation, or deprivation of the use of a limb, blindness, loss of an eye, or other permanent disability or unintentional death" (Winter 1994, 943).

A controversial case arose in 1990 when a native African father went against his French wife's wishes and arranged their daughter's circumcision. On appeal, the father was given a five-year suspended sentence. Up to that point, all of the French cases had prosecuted immigrant parents—almost exclusively mothers—for the circumcisions of their daughters. The first trial against a circumcisor occurred in 1991, and an unprecedented three-year prison sentence was handed down. France has been exceptional among Western countries in prosecuting FGC cases.

Although it received considerable press coverage in the United States, FGC never became a prominent issue here. Fran Hosken introduced the issue to the West with her report on the practice in 1979. She coined the term "female genital mutilation" (Messito 1997–98). In the same year, feminist Daly (1978) highlighted FGC as one of several "sadistic" rituals designed to oppress women. The first major U.S. news story describing FGC appeared in 1980 (Dullea 1980). For the next decade, only a few new articles appeared each year (Hoeschen 1999). In 1992 Alice Walker published *Possessing the Secret of Joy,* a fictional account of an African woman's circumcision experience (Messito 1997–98). Soon, *Warrior Marks,* Walker's coauthored nonfictional account of FGC, and a related documentary film, followed the novel. Abe Rosenthal at the *New York Times* began featuring in-depth special reports on the practice in 1995.

Eventually, the publicity generated by these individuals (and others) had an impact. In 1993, Representative Patricia Schroeder

(Democrat-Colorado) introduced anti-FGC legislation, and Canada made FGC grounds for asylum (Messito 1997–98). Senator Henry Reid (Democrat-Nevada) signed on as a cosponsor of the legislation after learning about FGC from CNN's Egyptian broadcast (Messito 1997–98). The U.S. law criminalizing FGC was passed on September 30, 1996. It was part of a large Department of Defense Omnibus Appropriations Bill (Public Law No. 104-208, 110 Stat. 3009-708, 1996).

As noted in the last chapter, it seems that the United States failed to adopt a law sooner because legislators perceived that the practice was extremely rare in the nation. Instead, when legislation was ultimately passed in the United States, international factors appeared to play an important role in the process. One motivating factor appears to have been concern over asylum requests. The case of Fauziya Kassindja was critical in this regard. After her father's death, 17-year-old Kassindja fled Togo to avoid FGC at the hands of her remaining relatives. Kassindja's request for asylum became a news story when the Immigration and Naturalization Service (INS) held her in custody for two years before deciding her case. Although her request for asylum was initially denied by an immigration official, the denial was overturned on appeal and she was granted permission to stay in the country. The INS was clearly concerned that if Kassindja were granted asylum, another "eighty million" African women would also become eligible. In their brief to the Board of Immigration Appeals, the INS attorneys cautioned that "the Board . . . cannot simply grant asylum to all who might be subjected to a practice deemed objectionable or a violation of a person's human rights" (*In re Kasinga* [sic], 1996 BIA LEXIS 15, 32).

Kassindja's case was the first successful gender-based asylum claim in the United States (Gunning 1999). The Board of Immigration Appeals rejected the INS argument. The majority of the board's members argued that they could consider the facts of only the case before them and that a consideration of future cases would inappropriately constitute policymaking. In this way, they indirectly called on the federal legislature to take action.

Three considerations form the primary basis for asylum in the United States. People must demonstrate (1) that they are fleeing persecution, (2) that the persecution is based on race, religion, nationality, membership in a particular social group, or political opinion, and (3) that if they are deported, harm will be unavoidable. Applicants must also be credible. With respect to each factor, the Board of Immigration Appeals found in favor of Kassindja. The case was a milestone, because it was the first successful gender-based asylum claim in the United States. The Kassindja appeal was decided in the spring of 1996.

The related case of Lydia Oluloro, from Nigeria, occurred shortly after the Kassindja appeal. Oluloro had already experienced FGC but sought asylum to protect her two daughters from the practice. She successfully argued that if she was forced to return to Nigeria, she would have to take them with her, and they would almost certainly be circumcised.

The U.S. federal legislature passed its anti-FGC law in November 1996. Based on this timing, it appears that the asylum cases were at least part of the motivation behind the U.S. legislation. As noted above, a key component in seeking asylum is that harm would be unavoidable if a person were returned to the home country. This claim would be difficult to make against African countries that had anti-FGC laws and eradication policies. In tying U.S. foreign aid to other countries' eradication efforts, some in the federal legislature may have been trying to prevent a tide of African women from seeking asylum on American shores.

Given this background, it is not surprising that the U.S. law is more outwardly focused than either the Egyptian health decree or the Tanzanian law. The U.S. law targets countries where the practice occurs. Before the bill was passed, newspaper editorials highlighted the law's international importance. For example, Joan Beck argued that the Schroeder bill should be supported, not only because of its effect in the United States but also "because of the message it would send to countries where the practice is common."[4] Abe Rosenthal suggested a program in which 1 percent of U.S. foreign aid would be committed to the eradication of FGC globally.[5] The final law was indeed explicitly international in character. It did three things: (1) it banned FGC in the United States, (2) it linked foreign aid and support for loans from international organizations to countries' FGC eradication efforts, and

(3) it made education about the practice mandatory for all new immigrants. (The law was later revised to limit mandatory education to immigrants from countries where the practice is prevalent.) Thus, two out of the three objectives of the law were directed at foreign governments or individuals arriving from foreign countries.

In the United States, as in other Western countries, the anti-FGC law applied primarily to a marginalized, relatively powerless group —immigrants from Africa. Because FGC is very rare in the United States, the U.S. law served to reaffirm American traditions while "othering" African women (see, e.g., Gunning 1990–91; Obiora 1997; James 1998; Matua 2001). When particular practices distinguish members of different cultures, those practices may become symbols of social status, identifying a hierarchy of lifestyles (Gusfield 1986). In the discussion of functionality, I noted how the U.S. law is largely symbolic. The law regulates a group with little political or economic power in the United States—recent immigrants and refugees. The reaction of Americans to FGC was "incredulous and categorical condemnation" (Gunning 1990–91). The extent to which the American battle over FGC was a reaffirmation of traditional American values is illustrated by the situation of Harborview Hospital in Seattle, Washington.

Harborview serves a largely immigrant clientele. Many of its patients are Somali immigrants or refugees. Initially, the hospital refused pregnant women's requests that their daughters be circumcised. After lengthy discussions with refugee men and women, however, the hospital determined that its refusal was likely to do more harm than good. It appeared that if the hospital did not intervene, girls would be sent back to Somalia or would visit one of the three local midwives to be cut. Under these alternatives, the chances that the girls would experience the most severe form of FGC—infibulation—increased. Consequently, in September 1996, Harborview offered a compromise position: the hospital would nick the hood of a girl's clitoris in a procedure meant to draw blood but with no tissue removal or scarring (Coleman 1999). A local anesthetic would be used, and the procedure would be performed on only girls old enough to understand the procedure and give consent (informed parental consent was also required). The belief was that this medically safe procedure would provide an alternative to more dangerous and invasive forms of FGC. In fact, while some forms of FGC are more comparable to male castration than male circumcision, the procedure proposed by Harborview was somewhat less invasive than male circumcision because no tissue would be removed.

The Harborview compromise was never implemented because the hospital was "besieged by outraged opponents" (Coleman 1999, 745). The hospital was inundated with letters and phone calls protesting the compromise. Opponents suggested that "even talking about cutting female genitals legitimizes a barbaric practice" (Coleman 1999, 747). A Harborview physician who claimed it was "imperative that we try to understand the cultural practices of other people and that we respect privacy of families and their physicians" (Coleman 1999, 748) received hate mail and death threats for weeks. Apparently, it was not the harmful physical consequences but the practice itself that riled the American public. An obstetrician/gynecologist at Harborview suggested that, as an unfortunate result of the failed compromise, the hospital was likely to find itself dealing with the medical and psychological repercussions of midwives' work in the near future. The Harborview Hospital experience suggests that Americans see FGC not only as harmful to the girls who undergo the procedure but also as a threat to American ideals of gender equality.

Rather than resist international norms, Westerners enthusiastically embraced them—to the point of assertively challenging any hint of deviation from those norms. The manner in which the United States targeted FGC reinforced the "superiority" of Western values in the global system.

Same Words, Different Meanings

The point of this analysis has been to develop a theory of "glocalization," that is, the interaction of the global and the local. The diffusion of laws and policies around the globe can mask important differences in the meaning and implications of policies for different countries. This research provides a first step in that direction. How the seemingly "universal" principles that Westerners take for granted are contested locally provides important insights into how power operates globally (cf. Silbey 1997; Maurer 1997).

It appears that functionality and international standing combine to influence the level of conflict generated by reform efforts. Functionality is necessary to generate conflict; when a policy has functional relevance, international standing exacerbates conflict. The greatest level of conflict occurred in Egypt, a country with some power in the international system and in which an anti-FGC policy had functional relevance. The United States, where an anti-FGC policy had little direct effect on the public, had the lowest level of conflict.

As expected, more contestation coincides with less public input into the policymaking process. At the national level, reform is often a top-down process (see also Edelman 1964, 172). National laws are developed to change rather than reflect local attitudes. Further, despite the consistency of legalization across countries, there was some important variation in national strategies. In Egypt, the local community figured into the process—but, somewhat oddly, as an element that had to be "worked around." Egypt was forced to forgo formal legislation that would involve its representative body, and it opted for a more bureaucratic policy. While the United States and Tanzania have formal laws, Egypt has only a health ministry decree against FGC. This demonstrates that leaders faced with high levels of opposition may attempt to avoid formal parliamentary proceedings.

The case of Tanzania illustrated how state leaders may emphasize global consensus and adopt the discourse of international actors when a policy might fuel domestic interethnic disputes. The state in Tanzania must consistently demonstrate its neutrality to the various ethnic groups that make up the country's population. To do this, Tanzanian leaders embraced international calls to abolish FGC and aligned themselves closely with international actors. This contrasted with opponents of FGC in Egypt, who became more persuasive locally by *distancing* themselves from international actors.

Apathy in the United States, opposition in Egypt, and political considerations in Tanzania were influential in delaying the adoption of policies to eradicate FGC. All of these countries adopted policies late in the diffusion process. It appears that functional relevance can slow down the adoption process by generating a serious debate over the value of a policy. Ironically, functional *ir*relevance can produce a similar effect because individuals are not highly motivated to deal with the problem.

The United States provided one instance of how these policies may be more "extranationally" directed in the West than in the periphery. In the case of FGC, although all three countries adopted similar policies around the same time, the U.S. law was substantially more international. Not only did the law ban FGC in the United States; it also linked foreign aid to eradication efforts in other countries. In contrast, the Egyptian and Tanzanian policies were entirely local.

Taking the United States and Egypt as examples, although both countries adopted anti-FGC "laws" in response to the growing international sentiment opposing the practice, the meaning of the laws in the two countries was quite different. The substance of the laws in Egypt and the United States illustrates how elites assigned different meaning to eradication efforts in the two countries. In December 1995, Health Minister Ali Abel Fattah of Egypt issued his decree banning FGC in all public hospitals in Egypt. His successor, Health Minister Ismail Sallam, extended the ban to all medical practitioners in July 1996.[6] The decree was directed at a fairly elite group of Egyptians—doctors. Furthermore, all classes of Egyptians practice FGC, so the ban affected the upper as well as the lower classes in the country. No aspect of the health decree was focused outside the borders of Egypt.

In comparison, the U.S. policy on FGC was more externally directed. The U.S. policy attempted to influence African states and even international migratory flows. The Egyptian policy was entirely domestic. At the most fundamental level, this difference suggests one way in which American hegemony operates. Although from one vantage point, the international diffusion of anti-FGC legislation makes it appear that eradicating FGC was a consensual goal of many nations, from another, the power relations involved are decidedly more pronounced (cf. Edelman et al. 1999; Waters 1995).

The meaning of policies adopted as a result of international diffusion also appears to be very different in Egypt and the United States. Specifically, the U.S. policy reaffirms traditional values, but a similar policy in Egypt distances the state from traditional values. The international (and U.S.) pressure on countries to eliminate FGC has thus far met with limited success on the ground (Carr 1997). One unfortunate consequence of the limited erosion of the practice is that, in countries like Egypt, the government is forced to choose between the traditions of its local constituency and international norms. In other words, the international norm against FGC forced the Egyptian state to distance itself from its local citizenry.

Unlike the anti-FGC norm, many international norms are not targeted toward individual behavior. For example, the diffusion of science ministries in the middle of the twentieth century did not directly impinge on any local cultural practice (see Finnemore 1996). The adoption of science ministries may therefore have been more pro forma across countries than the adoption of anti-FGC policies. Likewise, international norms may target individual behavior that is consistently found in all countries. For these norms (e.g., against gender inequality [see Berkovitch 1999b]), policy adoption and enforcement may be consistently contested across countries.

. . . .

SEVEN

Individual Response

A Clash of Alternative Meaning Systems

We do not believe that force changes traditional habits and practices. Su-
perior Western attitudes do not enhance dialogue or equal exchange of ideas.
—Seble Dawit and Salem Mekuria, "The West Just Doesn't Get It," 1993

Taken-for-granted "truths" at the international level are not necessarily truths in the communities where FGC has been passed down
through generations. For example, although most Muslims agree that
Islam does not require FGC, the Mandinga in Guinea-Bissau disagree.
Members of this ethnic group trace the origins of the practice back
to the Prophet Mohammed. They related the following story to eth-
nographer Michelle Johnson (2000). Mohammed's first wife was too
old to have children, so he took a younger second wife. After some
time, his first wife became jealous of the beautiful new bride. While
Mohammed was away on a trip, she pierced the ears of the younger
wife. Because only slaves had pierced ears at the time, the first wife was
hoping that Mohammed would reject his new wife when he discovered
the piercing. When Mohammed returned home, he heard from God
through an intermediary that he should not worry about his young
wife's pierced ears. God told him the piercing was beautiful and soon
all the women would begin to pierce their ears in the same way. And
indeed, when the other women saw the new wife with gold in her ears,
they began to pierce their own ears. Eventually, Mohammed had to
leave on another trip. This time his first wife clipped off the younger
wife's clitoris. Once again, when Mohammed returned an intermediary came to him and conveyed a message from God. The intermediary
told Mohammed that the circumcision would make the young wife

even more lovely and pure. The Mandinga related this story to explain why they circumcised their daughters.

When Johnson asked a Koranic scholar and holy man whether the Koran actually contained such a passage, he explained that the story was a "secret" passage: "Even experts are not always perceptive enough to see or understand all the mysteries of the *Qu'ran*" (Johnson 2000, 221). He and the rest of the community believed the story was real. It did not matter that the story had not been formally recorded in the collections of Mohammed's teachings. As this example illustrates, Westerners might be missing the importance of secrecy and hidden meanings in some African cultures when they claim that there is no "real" textual basis for FGC.

The perspective of international actors as they began to fight actively against FGC stood in stark contrast to the perspective of many individuals in the communities where FGC was practiced. Local political and religious leaders in some communities have supported FGC. Often, the practice has been linked to nationalism. Jomo Kenyatta, the first president of Kenya, condoned the practice and warned that the abolition of FGC would "prevent the Gikuyu from perpetuating that spirit of collectivism and national solidarity which they have been able to maintain from time immemorial" (Kenyatta 1978, first published in 1938, 135). Some local communities were strongly supportive of the practice even when the international community was adamantly opposed. In these communities, the practice was sometimes so taken for granted that it was difficult for women to imagine *not* being circumcised.

Most of the literature on FGC considers individuals—why they practice FGC, how it affects them, and whether they are likely to change the tradition. This chapter also focuses on individuals, but rather than attempt a summary of that entire body of literature here, I focus on the theme of this book: how institutional conflict played itself out at this, the most concrete of levels.

At the international level, conflict over FGC was procedural. In determining whether they should intervene, international organizations contrasted the idea of national sovereignty with the idea of universal human rights. At the national level, the conflict was also procedural. Here, the process of representative democracy was pitted against universal human rights. In both cases, the goal of universal human rights was assumed. The questions (although never explicitly asked) were whether circumventing national sovereignty and representative democracy would result in the more effective pursuit of universal human rights.

In contrast, at the individual level, the conflict between local and international institutions is substantive. The debate is over not two valued but contradictory ideas supported by the same system but rather two completely different systems. This results in several consequences. First, local culture can provide a particularly powerful source of resistance to the ideas of the international system (Babatunde 1998, 179–82). Second, compromise over the practice becomes more feasible at the individual level than at the national or international level. For example, at the international level, the relationship between Islam and FGC is settled: Islam does not require the practice. The relationship between Islam and FGC is not nearly that clearly defined within some individual communities. Other examples of compromise include medicalizing the procedure or adopting a milder form of it. These outcomes were explicitly unacceptable at the international level.

To elaborate on these points, I rely heavily on an analysis of Demographic and Health Survey (DHS) data[1] from several African countries that I conducted with Mayra Gómez and Barbara McMorris (2002).[2] Specifically, we asked which women in African countries where FGC is common are opposed to the practice and have elected not to circumcise their daughters. In the next chapter, I will discuss a related analysis of DHS surveys that asks the follow-up question: When African women oppose FGC, what explanations do they give for their opposition? DHS data are not yet available from every country where FGC is practiced. In addition, surveys are slightly different across countries. In Egypt, Kenya, Mali, Niger, and Sudan, women were asked whether they favored the continuation of FGC and whether they had circumcised or planned to circumcise their eldest daughter. Those countries provide the basis for the analysis in this chapter. A question regarding why women opposed FGC was asked in Egypt, Kenya, Mali, Niger, and Sudan as well as in the Central African Republic. Those countries provide the basis for the analysis in the next chapter. In both analyses, we controlled for both region and country so that the individual-level analyses could be compared and conceptually connected.

In terms of what affects attitudes and behaviors with respect to FGC, we looked at a number of factors but were particularly interested in the effect of religion. Because it is central to identity, religion is likely to be a key determinant of the *salience* of international norms for women. Religion provides a transcendent explanation for action that bolsters individuals' choice of "traditional" norms instead of international norms. Islam has served as a base of resistance to a number of global norms. The global system itself arises from Christian countries, so Christian women's ideology is more consistent with the international ideals. Because Christian women are more likely to identify with the Western ideas carried by the international system, we also expected to find that the effect of exposure to Western discourse—college and public media—would be greater for Christians than for Muslims.

Our analysis revealed that Christianity is a strong predictor of rejecting FGC—in both attitudes and behavior. In addition, we found evidence that anti-FGC ideas among college-educated women are more influential for Christians. Likewise, the mass media has more impact on discouraging the practice among Christian women than Muslim women. It is not sufficient for individuals to be exposed to the norms of the international system. Exposure to Western ideas appears to work better if it is accompanied by a meaning system that is supportive of those ideas. Local culture can provide an alternative meaning system for women, providing the scripts for resisting or accepting international FGC reform efforts.

Islam in Local Communities

At the local level, there is evidence that the relationship between Islam and FGC extends beyond explicit statements in Islamic texts. The story from the Mandinga in Guinea-Bissau is one example of this. On the other side of the African continent, Ellen Gruenbaum also encountered a connection between Islam and FGC (1991). She found that in Sudan, proximity to high-status Islamic groups increased the likelihood of the practice. Gruenbaum studied two communities in Somalia in 1989: the Kenana, who practiced infibulation, and the Zabarma, who practiced a much milder form of FGC. The two groups worked together in a community that had been formed by the government. The Kenana were considered by all to be the higher-status group because of their closer connection to the Islamic world. After interacting in close proximity to the Kenana for a decade, the Zabarma began to adopt many of the practices of their higher-status neighbors, including the more extreme form of FGC. These cases illustrate the presence of alternative meaning systems at the local level that are not replicated in the international system. Below, I relate our findings on the impact of religion, as well as other factors, on whether women favored the continuation of FGC and whether they circumcised their daughters.

Empirical Background

The recent increase in international data on FGC has led to many new empirical studies of the practice (e.g., Williams and Sobieszczyk 1997). Specifically, recent DHS modules on FGC offer a unique opportunity to evaluate changes in an individual behavior that has been targeted for change by the international community. The nationally representative surveys were administered in local languages and used locally recognized terminology. The surveys in Egypt, Kenya, Mali, Niger, and Sudan[3] asked women a series of questions about FGC, including (1) whether they favor the continuation of the practice, and (2) whether they have circumcised or intend to circumcise their daughters. Despite the sensitivity of the questions, there was no evidence that women refused to answer or that the results were biased toward particular responses. Because mothers are primarily responsible for having their daughters circumcised, the surveys focused on their attitudes and behavior as an indication of change in rates of FGC.

I briefly describe some of the countries' key similarities and differences here (U.S. Central Intelligence Agency 1999; Information Please Almanacs 1999). I have discussed Egypt at length elsewhere but incorporate some basic additional information on that country.

Because the Central African Republic is included in the next chapter's analysis, I also describe its basic characteristics to provide a point of reference. National statistics are provided in table 7.1. In the modern historical context, all of the countries have experienced European colonization or occupation.

The Central African Republic, Mali, and Niger were French colonies that claimed independence in the early 1960s. Kenya was a British colony but became fully independent in 1963. Britain occupied Egypt until 1953 (following a history of occupation by Turks and then an Anglo-French coalition). Egypt and Britain jointly administered Sudan until 1953 under a "condominium agreement" signed in 1899. Recent histories thus hold a common theme of occupation and colonization, although the colonial powers involved were different.

With respect to women's rights, all of the countries except Sudan have laws or constitutional provisions that call for gender equality (although Kenya only recently amended its constitution to prohibit gender discrimination). In Sudan, the government maintains the Public Order Police, who are commissioned to enforce proper social behavior, including restrictions on "immodest dress" by women. Gender segregation is also common in social settings in Sudan. In the other countries, laws mandating gender equality are largely decoupled from practice and are often inconsistent with more specific laws, such as those regarding marriage, inheritance, and travel. In the countries where Islam is the dominant religion, actual practice tends to coincide with Islamic beliefs regarding women's proper role in society. For example, in Egypt and Kenya, women must have the permission of their fathers or husbands to obtain a passport. In all of the countries, it appears that girls are more likely than boys to drop out of school because of the pressure to begin families, and there is strong social pressure against women working outside the home.

With respect to current political and economic conditions, Egypt is the most developed country, followed by Kenya. The life expectancy for a person in Egypt is six years greater than that of the next highest country, its fertility rate is the lowest of the six countries, and its GDP per capita is nearly double that of the next highest country. Sudan is the most unstable of the six countries. Twenty years of civil war be-

Table 7.1 Background Statistics for the Central African Republic (CAR), Egypt, Kenya, Mali, Niger and Sudan

	CAR	Egypt	Kenya	Mali	Niger	Sudan
Populations (millions)	3.44	67.0	28.8	10.43	9.96	34.48
Land (square kilometers)	622,980	1.00 million	583,000	1.24 million	1.27 million	2.51 million
Infant mortality (per 1,000 live births)	103	67	59	119	113	71
Life expectancy (years)	47	62	47	48	42	56
Fertility rate (children per woman)	5.0	3.3	3.9	7.0	7.2	5.6
Gross domestic product per capita (purchasing power parity, $)	1,640	2,850	1,550	790	970	930
Male literacy rate (percent)	68.5	63.6	86.3	39.4	20.9	57.7
Female literacy rate (percent)	52.4	38.8	70.0	23.1	6.6	34.6

Source: U.S. Central Intelligence Agency 1999.

tween the north and the south have claimed 1.5 million lives, more than 4 percent of the country's total population. In Niger, a group of army officers overthrew the elected government in 1996 and continue to hold power. The Central African Republic is also relatively unstable (U.S. Department of State 2000). The president, Ange Felix Patasse, was first elected in 1993 and won reelection in 1999 by a narrow margin. The military's loyalty to Patasse is questionable (many members of the military mutinied in 1996). In 2000, Patasse dissolved that branch of the military responsible for domestic security and created a new Special Presidential Unit. From 1998 to 2000, a special U.N. peacekeeping force was present in the country.

In contrast, Kenya held its first multiparty elections since independence in 1992; the most recent elections were held in 1997. The governments in both Egypt and Mali have also been relatively stable, although religious tensions in both countries have led to numerous deaths in recent years. Economically, Mali, Niger, and Sudan are the poorest countries. All of the countries tend to rely on international donors to fund gender equality and children's welfare programs because the governments lack the resources to fund social programs internally.

Despite Western interpretations of the practice, not circumcising one's daughters is considered deviant in many regions of these countries. FGC is practiced on nearly all girls in Egypt. Sudan and Mali also have high rates of FGC: 89 percent and 94 percent, respectively. The rate is lower but still substantial in Kenya (about 37 percent) (Carr 1997). Approximately half of the women in the Central African Republic have been circumcised. In contrast, in Niger, FGC has always been a minority tradition. In Niger, the percentage of women who have experienced FGC is about 14 percent. Infibulation, the most extreme form of FGC, is the most common form in Sudan, while excision is more common in Egypt, Kenya, Mali, and Niger. Although the governments in the six countries formally oppose FGC, the degree of specific action against the practice has varied. As noted earlier, in Kenya FGC was historically linked to nationalist movements; it was a plank in the anticolonial platform of the 1930s, and the founding father of the country explicitly linked FGC to nationalist pride.

Sudan legally banned FGC in 1974, but the practice continues to be widespread there. In fact, there are reports that women displaced from the south as a result of the war are having their daughters circumcised even if they themselves had not experienced the practice. The Central African Republic adopted an ordinance against FGC in 1996. Mali and Niger adopted anti-FGC policies only recently. Neither government has proposed legislation prohibiting FGC, but both support educational efforts to eliminate the practice and provide media access to proponents of its elimination. In 1997, the Ministry for the Promotion of Women in Mali created a National Committee against Violence towards Women that links all the international organizations active in preventing FGC in Mali. Likewise, the Niger government has been cooperating with UNICEF to eradicate the practice. International organization involvement in eradication efforts is extensive in all of the countries.

Earlier, we described how the Egyptian government reissued and expanded a health ministry decree to ban the performance of any type of FGC in public health clinics in 1994. The reissued decree came under political and legal attack by Islamic fundamentalists. Their legal claim was that the decree went against Islam, the state religion. Ultimately, national courts upheld the decree on the ground that Islam does not require FGC. Since then, a discussion of FGC and its dangers has been added to the curriculum of the Egyptian school system. Television programs condemn the practice there. Kenya's current president has issued two presidential decrees banning FGC. In 1996, anti-FGC legislation was proposed in Kenya but failed to pass. Nevertheless, explicit anti-FGC policies are in place in all of the countries.

Internal versus External Modernization

Under a neoinstitutionalist framework, individuals, like states, derive their identities from a system of institutionalized values, actions, and beliefs. I have already noted that it is possible for different and contradictory institutions to exist simultaneously. Although FGC is an institution in some settings, opposition to FGC is consistent with the principles institutionalized in the international system. The point at which institutions contradict is a critical point for creating change. A salient awareness of the contradiction is a precursor to change, however. One of the reasons the West did not act sooner with respect to FGC is that most Westerners had never heard of the practice. They were shocked to learn that such a practice occurred; it was antithetical to many ideas that they take for granted.

Likewise, individuals operating within systems where FGC is institutionalized will not abandon the practice unless they realize that FGC is not institutionalized everywhere. One key empirical factor, then, that links macro and micro levels is the exposure of these individuals to the powerful scripts embedded in the international system. Exposure alone is insufficient to generate change, however. In addition to exposure, those individuals must find some salience in the alternative institutions. Individuals who practice FGC will have to sufficiently identify with the international system to imagine that its perspective on FGC has some legitimacy and relevance to them.

A related, alternative explanation for change is suggested by modernization theories (Inkeles and Smith 1974; Inglehart and Baker 2000). According to modernization theories, exposure to modern structures leads individuals to adopt a particular type of personality, emphasizing rationality and secular beliefs. For example, Bell explains that during the process of industrialization, individuals move from a state of war against nature to a state of war against "fabricated nature" (Bell 1976, 1973). As part of this process, individuals begin to emphasize materialism over religion, and, ultimately, self-expression over materialism (see also Etzioni 2000). From this perspective, change is less about institutional conflict and more about the functional evolution of values.

Modernization theorists have been critiqued for implying that Western notions of the world are somehow more "evolved" than other perspectives and for placing the blame for underdevelopment on the victims of imperialism. Although these assumptions are present in some modernization texts, they are not essential to modernization theory. Divorced from such assumptions, modernization theory suggests a powerful, interesting, and empirically testable process. Is there something about an individual's relationship to nature that fundamentally affects his or her worldview?

There is a great deal of similarity in the predictions of neoinstitutionalism and modernization theories because many of the structures that accompany modernization also carry the scripts of the international system. The fundamental difference is that neoinstitutionalists imagine reform as a top-down process in which international ideas become the basis for action and reform. In contrast, modernization theorists give primacy to the national level, arguing that national development and accompanying structural changes affect individual values by altering the relationship of individuals to their environment. National industrialization inevitably leads to individual modernization, and the process is largely independent of the nation's relationship to other countries or the global system. The modernization of populations is primarily a process of *national* development, not *international* diffusion. Inkeles refers to this as an "internal" explanation for modernization (Inkeles 1998, xv).

This contrasts with neoinstitutionalists' idea that change is externally scripted by the international system. From this perspective, forces external to any particular nation-state influence the overall course of all nation-states and, to some extent, the people within them. For neoinstitutionalists, individuals will change their attitudes and behaviors to conform to international norms when they are familiar with the institutional logic of the international system. Privileging exposure in this way leads to hypothesized effects from those aspects of modernity that specifically carry the scripts of the international system. Both types of theorists would expect education, employment, and media exposure to influence attitudes, but modernization theorists would expect more effect for development per se. To determine the conditions under which global institutions, already evident in national policies, come to affect individual attitudes and behavior, Barbara McMorris, Mayra Gómez, and I (2002) used the ideas of "internal" and "external" modernization as a starting point.

In our statistical analysis of DHS data, we used hierarchical modeling techniques to determine how women's personal situations as well as their regional and national environments influenced their attitudes toward FGC and decisions to circumcise their daughters. With respect to these questions, we conducted two separate analyses—one predicting attitudes toward continuation of FGC, the other predicting the actual behavior of circumcising one's daughter. This dual analysis bol-

Table 7.2 Attitudes toward FGC among Women in The Central African Republic, Egypt, Kenya, Mali, Niger, and Sudan

Country	Circumcised (%)	Favor FGC (%)	Oppose FGC (%)	No Opnion (%)
Central African Republic	43	30	56	14
Egypt	97	82	13	6
Kenya	38	20	73	7
Mali	94	75	13	12
Niger	5	10	90	—
Sudan	89	79	21	—

Some figures do not add to exactly 100 because of rounding.
Source: Demographic and Health Surveys.

stered the reliability of our findings and allowed us to explore differences in how attitudes and behaviors are influenced.

There is evidence of some erosion in the occurrence of FGC at the individual level. Table 7.2 shows a modest reduction in the intergenerational continuity of the practice in a sample of women from the Central African Republic, Egypt, Kenya, Mali, Niger, and Sudan. With the exception of Niger, all of the countries show that fewer women favor FGC than have actually been circumcised. Although the percentage favoring FGC is very high in several countries, it is considerably less than perfect intergenerational reproduction. Predictably, our measure of intergenerational stability, a woman's own circumcision experience, had the most powerful impact on both her behavior and her attitude toward FGC.

Predicting Individual Attitudes and Actions

For individual attitude and behavior change to occur, both modernization theories and neoinstitutionalism point to the importance of factors that simultaneously carry the scripts of the international system and accompany national development (or modernization). We hypothesized that these factors—education, mass media, and working outside the home—would affect women's attitudes and behavior with respect to FGC. For education, the media, and employment, these hypotheses were confirmed.

Both education and the media are Western constructs, and both tend to be carriers of Western ideas in the developing world (Inkeles 1996; Ramirez and Boli 1987; Herman and McChesney 1997, 8). Thus, higher levels of education and media exposure are likely associated with less favorable attitudes toward targeted traditional practices. Both years of education and attending college (a benefit attained by only 2.6 percent of the women in our sample) had significantly negative effects on the probability that women favored the continuation of FGC or circumcised their daughters. Each year of basic education decreased the probability that a woman would circumcise her daughters by 15 percent and decreased the likelihood of preferring FGC continuation by 16 percent. For those few who did experience college, the correlation with opposition to FGC was very pronounced. Women who had not attended college were about seven times more likely to circumcise their daughters and about five times more likely to favor FGC continuation than college attendees. Owning a radio also decreased the likelihood of practicing FGC by 20 percent and favorable attitudes by 27 percent.

Employment was also an important factor. Modernization theorists have demonstrated that nonagricultural employment is a source of materialist or postmaterialist values for men (Inkeles 1996). The same is likely to be true for women. Women who work outside the home are also more likely to be exposed to the scripts of the international system. In addition, in societies where FGC is practiced, women typically acquire value through marriage. A failure to be circumcised can drastically reduce a woman's chances of marriage. However, women who earn money outside the home may have other avenues to future security. Thus, increasing women's economic independence should lead to a decrease in onerous marriage requirements (see also Toubia and Izett 1998). We therefore predicted that women who work for pay outside the home would be less likely to favor the continuation of FGC or to circumcise their daughters than women who did not work outside the home. Our results supported this prediction; working outside the home for pay decreased the likelihood that a woman circumcised her daughter by 43 percent and decreased the probability of favoring continuation of the practice by 33 percent.

Some modernization theorists have emphasized the importance of urban dwelling on the erosion of traditional social practices, but the empirical results have been mixed for this factor (Inkeles 1971). Living in an urban area increases the chances of being exposed to scripts from the international system. For example, the "Westernizing" effects of education and the mass media are more likely to indirectly reach an urban family than a rural family, even if the family is itself poorly educated or lacks a radio. Consequently, we expected women in urban areas to be less likely to favor the continuation of FGC or to circumcise their daughters than women in rural areas. In fact, we found that living in an urban area decreased the probability that a woman would favor the continuation of FGC by 36 percent but had no significant effect on behavior. When education, the media, employment, and the other factors are controlled, urban women are just as likely as rural women to circumcise their daughters. Living in a city led women to voice opposition to FGC, but urban women had not changed their behavior any more than rural women. We conclude that although urban dwelling is more likely than rural dwelling to expose women to the normative principles of the international system, the increased exposure may be minimal compared with the exposure resulting from more direct "norm carriers" such as education.

Modernization theorists have demonstrated that attitude change is possible among older as well as younger individuals (Inkeles 1971; Inglehart and Baker 2000). In Muslim countries, older married women have been found to have considerably more independence than younger married women (Geiger 1997; Gluckman 1955). Further, older women will have witnessed more circumcisions and may be more familiar with the complications that can ensue from the procedures. As a group, older women average less education than younger women, but when education was controlled, for the reasons just noted, we expected older women to express greater dissatisfaction with FGC. Although older women would be more likely to have circumcised their daughters, with respect to attitudes, we expected older women to be less likely to favor the continuation of FGC than younger women.

The hypothesized effect of age was statistically significant in both cases, and, as expected, the direction of the effect was reversed for the two dependent variables. Older women were *less* likely to favor the continuation of FGC, but each year of age increased the probability that a woman had circumcised or planned to circumcise her daughters by 6 percent. Older women may have circumcised their daughters before there was international opposition to the practice. The reverse effect for attitudes is consistent with prior findings and was predicted. Older women are accorded considerable independence in Muslim societies and thus are more able to question and critically evaluate societal norms. When all other factors are controlled, each year of age decreased by 1 percent the probability that a woman favored the continuation of FGC.

Resistance

Factors increasing resistance to "modern" ideas were commitment to Islam, rural dwelling, and agricultural employment (Inkeles 1971). Whether Islam requires FGC is a contested question (Boddy 1991). The practice predates Islam, does not occur in most Middle Eastern countries, and is not explicitly required by the Koran. Nevertheless, some powerful Islamic leaders advocate the practice, and in Africa its occurrence has historically coincided with the rise of Islam (see, e.g., Lancaster 1995). The Mandinga example at the beginning of the chapter illustrates how FGC can sometimes be viewed as a positive attribute of Islamic identity and culture. We therefore hypothesized that Christian women would be less likely than Muslim women to favor the continuation of FGC or to circumcise their daughters. As hypothesized, we found that Muslims and women of traditional African faiths were three times more likely to circumcise their daughters and four times more likely to favor the continuation of FGC than Christian women.

We also hypothesized that Christian women would find the anti-FGC message of international activists more salient than other women because the international norms would be more consistent with their overall view of the world. The interaction terms testing this proposition demonstrated an interesting effect. As expected, college-educated Christian women were significantly more likely to oppose FGC and not circumcise their daughters than either college-educated Muslims or non-college-educated Christians. As for the salience of messages from the mass media, our data suggested that media exposure had a stronger effect on behavior for Christian women than for Muslim women. However, religion did not affect the salience of mass media for attitudes. These findings suggest that media messages affect attitudes more easily than behavior. Exposure to media made Muslim women more likely to reject international norms behaviorally than attitudinally.

Neoinstitutionalism and modernization theories diverge in their predictions about the independent impact of modernization. We included three measures of modernization in our analysis—one for each level of analysis. At the individual level, we surmised that electricity could be an important predictor of individuals' perspectives on the world. Electricity represents a type of control over nature. Modernization theories suggest that controlling nature increases individuals' sense of instrumental self-efficacy. These individuals may thus feel empowered to reject traditional norms.

At the regional level, we created a development factor based on the percentage of men in nonagricultural occupations,[4] the percentage of literate people, and the percentage of people with electricity in the region.[5] Our expectation was that the greater the level of development in a region, the lower the probability that women in that region would favor the continuation of FGC or circumcise their daughters. Further, because Egypt is the most developed of the five countries considered, we initially hypothesized that in Egypt, women would have a lower probability of favoring the continuation of FGC or circumcising their daughters than women in the other four countries. However, in chapters 1 and 6, I described how critical factions in Egypt are resisting the eradication of FGC. Thus, there was reason to believe that this hypothesis would not be supported.

We expected, based on previous scholarship, that development would decrease the probability that women would favor the continuation of FGC or have their daughters circumcised. The results were quite interesting; the effect of development varied depending on the level of analysis considered. Electricity decreased the probability that a woman would favor the continuation of FGC by 29 percent but had no effect on behavior. Regional development, when all regions were considered, had no statistically significant effect on either attitudes or behavior. However, when we controlled for country, intranational regional development did correspond to reductions in the probabilities that women would favor the continuation of FGC or circumcise their daughters.

The most surprising finding was that women in Egypt—the most developed country—were *more* likely to favor circumcision or have their daughters circumcised than women in other countries. (The greater probability of favoring FGC in Egypt was statistically significant compared with all other countries; the greater probability of circumcising one's daughters was statistically significant compared with all other countries except Sudan, and even there the difference was in the same direction.)

Thus, regional development influences attitudes and behavior, but national resistance to international norms can outweigh the influence of regional development. Ironically, Egypt's relatively high level of development, when individual factors were controlled, may have allowed its overall population to be more resistant to the international norm against FGC than the populations of other countries. This is true despite Egypt's own national anti-FGC policy and health ministry decree. Of the five countries in our analysis, Egypt was in recent years the country with the most outspoken opponents to the international norm against FGC.

In sum, according to modernization theories and neoinstitutional theory, the key empirical factors that determine whether individual attitudes and behavior conform to international norms are education, the media, working outside the home, urban dwelling, and age. Modernization theories would also expect indicators of development to be important on their own. Religion was particularly important, both directly and indirectly, as a "translator" of the international anti-FGC message.

Scripts, Modernization, and Change

This chapter has considered the conditions under which individual behaviors and attitudes are consistent with world norms—norms already institutionalized in national policies. Based on a growing literature, we know that global institutions diffuse and become national policies. In the case of FGC, we also know that each of the five countries described here has an official state policy against the practice. The findings give some clue about the conditions that are necessary for this type of national policy to actually affect individual attitudes and behavior.

"Norm carriers"—education, college, the media, and employment —were factors directly associated with *both* intranational modernization and exposure to international norms. The college educated are distinct from others in their communities because of the worldview and relationship to the world that they develop growing up in elite households. Similarly, owning a radio may be an indicator that a person is part of a more rationalized, individualized cultural world than that of people who are so little plugged in to global systems that they lack radio access. College attendance and radio ownership were consistently associated with significant reductions in the probability that women in five African countries circumcised their daughters or favored the continuation of FGC. In other words, norm carriers influenced both attitudes and behavior with respect to a traditional practice targeted for change by the international community.

Factors associated with national modernity but less closely tied to norms—urban dwelling and electricity—affected attitudes but not behavior. We found that, all else being equal, women who lived in urban areas and whose households had electricity were more likely to say they opposed the continuation of FGC but were no less likely to have circumcised their daughters. The women in our sample circumcised their daughters in an earlier time period but were expressing current attitudes. Thus, this may indicate steps in a process of change where attitude change is followed by behavior change. Going forward, one might find that urban dwelling and electricity will begin to affect behavior as well as attitudes. Our findings suggest that internal modernization factors operate differently, perhaps more slowly, than norm carriers.

Christianity was a strong predictor of rejecting FGC—in both attitudes and behavior. In addition, we found evidence that anti-FGC ideas picked up in college were more influential for Christian women, suggesting that international ideals are more salient for some women than for others. Likewise, the mass media had more impact on behavior—discouraging the practice—among Christian women than among Muslim women. On the other hand, the effect of the mass media was equally influential on the *attitudes* of Christians and Muslims. These findings support the notion that alternative meaning systems, such as those provided by religion, can facilitate or impede the impact of carriers of world culture.

One of the most interesting findings was how the independent effect of modernization varied across levels of analysis. As noted above, whether a household had electricity influenced attitudes toward FGC but had no independent effect on behavior. At the regional level, regional development by itself had no effect on either attitudes or behavior. It was only when we introduced the categorical country variable that regional development had a significant negative effect on the probabilities of favoring FGC or circumcising one's daughter. Furthermore, the population in the most developed of our five countries, Egypt, when individual-level factors were controlled, was the most resistant to changing attitudes and behavior with respect to FGC.

EIGHT

Individual Frame Resonance

Explanations for Opposing
Female Genital Cutting

One of the most powerful tools was a film showing a woman who had not been mutilated giving birth. "People didn't understand that they could deliver a baby fairly easily."
—*Equality Now, "Around the World: Canada" (1997)*

In 1910 the Anglican Church founded two neighboring missionary stations—Kigare and Kabare—in Kenya (Murray 1976). Two Canadian brothers founded the stations, which followed a similar course for two decades. In January 1930, the bishop who oversaw these two stations issued a pastoral letter condemning FGC and requiring the church leaders to take disciplinary action against individuals who engaged in the practice. In Kigare, the then-current missionary (Reverend John Comely) was known for his caring love, his willingness to listen, and his unwillingness to compromise once he "received divine guidance." Upon receipt of the bishop's letter, Reverend Comely asked the church elders in his community to publicly renounce FGC. By 1931, he had the full support of the elders. With his backing, they issued a resolution calling for the excommunication of any church members who allowed FGC. Reaction was swift and far-reaching: "Schools went on strike, churches emptied and within a short time dissidents were commencing independent schools and conducting prayers separately" (Murray 1986, 99). Lands that had been donated to the church by clan members were reappropriated. The heavy-handed approach of church leaders drove parishioners away.

In Kabare, in contrast, church leaders devised a different strategy to deal with the bishop's letter. The missionary at that station, Reverend William Rampley, and his church elders came up with a compromise. Christian operators chosen by a committee of elders would circumcise both Christian boys and girls. A "modified" form of FGC would be carried out on the girls. (It is not clear whether this modified form was to be a *sunna* cutting or a mild clitoridectomy.) The ceremonies would be private and "disassociated with repugnant customs before and after" (Murray 1976, 100). Finally, to avoid offending non-Christians, the circumcised girl's uncle was to be given a goat after the circumcision, as was customary.

What was the outcome of the different strategies? Kigare today has a number of independent, breakaway churches. Although the Anglicans remained firm in their resolve against the practice there, their decision kept others from joining their church. Perhaps as a consequence, at the time Murray related the story, the rate of FGC was still quite high in the Kigare region (about 60 percent). At Kabare, the Christian circumcisor continued her work until the late 1930s. It was not until the 1940s, however, that Christian families (influenced by the East African Revival Movement) stopped circumcising their daughters. In that region, only 35 percent of girls are circumcised. There are many other historical factors that may be important in this discrepancy in the rates of FGC. Nevertheless, it seems possible that forcing changes inconsistent with local institutionalized values may have been counterproductive in Kigare and may explain why the overall rate of FGC is higher there than in Kabare.

In this chapter, I discuss Demographic and Health Survey data from the Central African Republic, Egypt, Kenya, Mali, and Sudan. The data indicate that when women oppose FGC, they gravitate toward explanations that are narrowly tailored to condemn the practice but not the cultural values that support it. As in the last chapter, I focus on the interconnection between international mobilization and local individuals.

The story here is one of "glocalization"—that is, tailoring a universal message to appeal to a local population (Robertson 1995; see also Silbey 1997).[1] Here, the question is to what extent the frames of international activists were "picked up" by local populations. The assumption of most social scientists, and anti-FGC activists as well, is that individuals agree with a reform when they find activists' strategic frames persuasive. This model imagines individuals consciously weighing the pros and cons of an action, ultimately undertaking that action if it provides sufficient benefits for them. A more top-down model—one consistent with neoinstitutional theory, might imagine that individuals do not stop to reflect on their actions but rather unconsciously engage in whatever action seems most "appropriate."

Once again using Demographic and Health Survey data, Kristin Carbone, Andrea Hoeschen, and I (2002) empirically tested these different conceptions of individual conformity to international norms. We found that the best explanation of individual attitudes toward FGC calls for an integration of the two perspectives. Specifically, when women in contexts where FGC was taken for granted opposed the practice, they tended to explicitly articulate the frames promoted by international activists. FGC opponents who had not been circumcised themselves and who lived in areas where the practice was rare were much less likely to use an international frame to explain their opposition; they tended to simply say that they opposed the practice because it was "bad." We also found that when women oppose FGC themselves but live in cultures that support FGC (cultures where most people are Muslim and the majority of women are circumcised), they tend to explain their opposition to the practice in the narrowest terms possible. Specifically, they are much more likely to adopt a medical explanation than an explanation that taps into notions of human rights. This suggests that at the individual level, even those women who agree with the international norm are concretely affected by local culture. Although culture manifests itself procedurally at the international level, determining strategy, it becomes increasingly substantive in terms of both acceptance and resistance as the conflict moves closer to the individual.

International Activist Frames

Master frames are "generic modes of punctuation, attribution, and articulation" that color or constrain numerous social movements (Snow and Benford 1992, 138). Swart (1995) suggests that a master frame is determined by its resonance with the cultural, political, and historical milieu in which it emerges. In other words, frames arise out of existing institutionalized principles. He notes that although the principles of the international system may be *perceived* as universal by the individuals enacting them, they are in fact rooted in specific times and places. For example, the current international privileging of economic progress, scientific knowledge, and individual human rights is Western in origin (Gaete 1991; Waters 1996; Gómez 2001).

There have been two key framing issues surrounding FGC. The first was whether to think of FGC in terms of sovereign autonomy or in terms of universal human rights. Did the problem of FGC justify international intervention in national politics? This question determined the role to be played by the international community in eradication efforts. As I have described, initial international efforts tended to emphasize sovereign autonomy, but more recent discourse has favored human rights. The second debate over framing was less about intervention and more about successful mobilization. Two master frames—scientific knowledge (in the form of medical information) and individual human rights—were prominent. Activists strategically framed opposition to FGC along these lines in ways they hoped would resonate with the targeted population—that is, mothers in the practicing cultures. In trying to persuade individuals to forgo the practice, they first relied on medical arguments but later adopted human rights themes. It is important to realize that at the same time activists were targeting groups of African mothers, they were also trying to capture the attention and sympathy of Western women and policymakers.

The framing strategies of international actors are uniquely clear in the case of FGC because of the previously mentioned joint statement of the World Health Organization (WHO), UNICEF, the U.N. Family Planning Association (UNFPA), and the U.N. Development Program (UNDP). The statement traced historic framing strategies and suggested a new alternative framing. From the 1960s through 1990, arguments against FGC were based entirely on a medical frame (WHO/UNICEF/UNFPA/UNDP 1995; U.N. Population Fund 1996).[2] The goal of international organizations during this time was primarily to reduce mortality and morbidity resulting from the practice. During this period, medical organizations were at the forefront of mobilization. For example, in 1977, the Sudanese Obstetrical and Gynecological Society sponsored one of the first meetings in post–World War II history on FGC (Boulware-Miller 1985). The International Planned Parenthood Federation, the International Organization of Gynecologists, and Doctors without Borders (as well as WHO) have also been very active opponents of FGC. In the United States, the American Medical Association, the American Women's Medical Association, and the American College of Obstetrics and Gynecology drafted policies opposing FGC (Boulware-Miller 1985). Further, a number of the most vocal anti-FGC activists—Nahid Toubia, Asma El Dareer, and Nawal El Saadawi—are doctors. As explained in chapter 3, prior to 1980, FGC was viewed as too culturally sensitive to use nonmedical arguments such as gender equality as a basis for change; the more "neutral" medical frame was dominant.[3]

In the 1990s, FGC came to be defined not only as a health problem but also as a violation of women's human rights (U.N. Population Fund 1996). The WHO/UNICEF/UNFPA/UNDP joint statement suggested that framing opposition to FGC in only medical terms had been a "mistake in policy strategy" (1995, 7). These organizations—which had been actively involved in eradication efforts—claimed that focusing on medical issues had led to two undesirable and counterproductive consequences. First, health professionals had tended to provide long lists of health consequences without distinguishing between the different types of FGC. For women who had undergone clitoridectomies (a milder form of circumcision), the health discourse, which typically included the consequences of infibulation, rang false. Second, the health discourse led some individuals to suggest that milder forms of circumcision, carried out under sterile conditions, would be acceptable.[4] The organizations considered this position untenable. Intending to include the broadest possible base of support, the recent mobilization by international organizations has linked in to both the medical and the human rights frames: "The argument against [FGC] takes its weight both from the basic issue of human rights and from the medical facts" (WHO/UNICEF/UNFPA/UNDP 1995, 1). The history of activism has been one of strategically choosing frames that activists believe are likely to resonate with African women.

Responses to International Framing

Is the assumption justified that individuals agree with a reform when they find activists' strategic frames persuasive? If this were true, based on the 1995 joint statement, we would expect medical and human rights explanations to be most prevalent among women in Africa who oppose FGC. On the other hand, the constructionist literature in sociology has convincingly demonstrated that individuals often express beliefs and take action not because they have carefully calculated the implications, costs, or benefits but because "people like them" have these beliefs and take these actions (March and Olsen 1998). In the case of FGC, when being uncircumcised becomes a mark of a "modern" individual, then women who are or aspire to be "modern" may oppose the practice without much articulation of why, indicating simply that the practice is "bad" or "backward." This is one possible source of disjuncture between collective action frames and individual opinions. Such a disjuncture may also arise when women oppose the practice independently of international actors. Women in remote areas of the world may agree with a social movement's goals without ever being exposed to the social movement or its strategic frames. Local activists, although they are likely aware of the WHO/UNICEF/UNFPA/UNDP joint statement, may choose to link their mobilization efforts to a unique script that appeals more to the individuals with whom they are interacting. Finally, individuals may simply not be very articulate or precise in their explanation about why they oppose the practice; they may believe in the frames put forward by the international organizations but not express them. For these reasons, we expect some individuals to articulate other explanations or no specific explanation at all for their opposition to FGC. Fundamentally, the nature and extent of explicit frame resonance among social movement adherents is an open question.

Complementing the powerful information on framing strategies derived from the 1995 joint statement, the Demographic and Health Survey modules on FGC again represent a unique opportunity to evaluate anti-FGC adherents' explanations for their opposition to the practice. The surveys in the Central African Republic, Egypt, Kenya,

Mali, and Sudan[5] asked women whether they favor the continuation of FGC and, if not, why not. Our sample included explicit and implicit adherents to the international anti-FGC movement—the women from the five countries who did not favor the continuation of FGC.[6] In other words, our analysis was based on a subsample that included only anti-FGC adherents.

The surveys used an open-ended question to determine why women opposed the continuation of FGC. Women were allowed to give multiple responses. Individuals administering the surveys assigned women's responses to one of nine[7] categories, including "other" and "do not know." Table 8.1 illustrates the distribution of women across all nine responses and also clustered into categories that coincide naturally with the two discourses suggested by the theoretical literature—that is, human rights and medical discourses—as well as a residual category that includes "constitutive" explanations (i.e., a woman says she opposes FGC simply because it is "bad"). As we noted, there are a number of ways to interpret the constitutive responses, including identity, apathy, ignorance, and so forth. This category provides an important contrast to medical and human rights explanations because all of the responses in this category share a lack of connection to international discourse. In the medical category, we included women who indicated that FGC caused medical complications or was painful. The human rights category included women who responded that FGC denied women's dignity or reduced sexual satisfaction.[8] In the constitutive category, we included women who responded that FGC was a bad tradition, was immoral, or was against their religion.[9]

Table 8.1 breaks down the explanations given by anti-FGC adherents in the Central African Republic, Egypt, Kenya, Mali, and Sudan. (Because women could give multiple responses, the total amounts are more than 100 percent.) The percentage of women giving a constitutive explanation was very high, 66 percent of all adherents. Constitutive explanations when unaccompanied by other types of explanations are particularly telling, and these percentages were also quite high. More than half of the uncircumcised adherents (58 percent) and more than one-fifth of the circumcised adherents (21 percent) em-

Table 8.1 Percentages of Anti-FGC Adherents Giving Medical (M), Human Rights (HR), or Constitutive (C) Explanations, by Circumcision Experience

Explanations for opposing FGC	Adherents Not Circumcised (N = 7,969)		Adherents Circumcised (N = 5,226)		Total, All Adherents
	Only Explanation (%)	Only or with Other Explanations (%)	Only Explanation (%)	Only or with Other Explanations (%)	Only or with Other Explanations (%)
Medical complications (M)	8	19	17	40	28
Painful experience (M)	2	8	6	24	14
Denying women's dignity (HR)	1	8	1	7	7
Reduces sexual satisfaction (HR)	1	5	3	12	8
Bad tradition (C)	36	56	13	31	46
Immoral (C)	1	3	1	3	3
Against my religion (C)	13	27	13	27	27
Other	6	8	2	5	7
Do not know	3	3	2	3	3
Combined categories					
Medical (M)	11	25	20	54	37
Human rights (HR)	3	18	3	12	14
Constitutive (C)	58	74	21	54	66

Note: Because multiple explanations were allowed, percentages total to more than 100.

ployed only a constitutive explanation for their opposition to FGC. Considering the ungrouped responses, the results are similar. For all women, the most common explanation was constitutive—that FGC is a bad tradition (66 percent). Thus, even for this widely discussed practice, explanations for opposition with no clear nexus to international frames were very common. Nevertheless, resonance with the frames of activists is also clearly present. In particular, 37 percent of women give a medical explanation for their adherence to the anti-FGC position.

The next question relating to explanations for opposition to FGC is which collective action frame is most persuasive. Snow and Benford note that elaborated master frames are more likely to be adopted by divergent social movements than restricted master frames (1992). A restricted frame is one that organizes a narrow band of ideas in a tightly interconnected manner (Snow and Benford 1992, 140). In the case of FGC, the medical frame is more restrictive because it addresses FGC in a compartmentalized fashion. By opposing FGC in technical medical terms, it does not address the history of the practice or the relationship of the practice to other practices or cultural constraints. An elaborated frame is organized in terms of a wide range of ideas that allows for extensive innovation and amplification. The human rights frame of anti-FGC activists is more elaborated than the medical frame because it allows numerous individuals to tap into it and because it can be applied to many cultural practices.

If the processes operate similarly at the movement level and the individual level, then one might expect explanations hinging on the more elaborated frame of human rights to be cited more frequently by movement adherents. This reasoning is consistent with the concern raised in the WHO/UNICEF/UNFPA/UNDP 1995 joint statement that the medical frame was too narrow and specific for combating FGC. The shift of these international organizations to a human rights frame is consistent with the idea that the more elaborated frame is more persuasive. On the other hand, the individual-level process might operate differently than the movement-level process. It may be that more specificity is a virtue at the individual level because people find concrete examples more meaningful than relatively vague generalizations. For example, a woman may be more persuaded to abandon the practice of FGC if she is told that it can result in serious hemorrhaging rather than that it is an affront to women's dignity.

In fact, we found that when women used one of the frames suggested by international activists, they were much more likely to use the medical frame. Very few women gave a human rights explanation for their opposition to FGC; only 18 percent of circumcised women and 19 percent of uncircumcised women cited harming women's dignity or reducing sexual satisfaction. In the responses for both groups, after "bad tradition," the next most common explanation for opposition to FGC was medical complications (28 percent). Further, 14 percent of adherents opposed FGC because they called it a painful experience. Although the human rights framing was promoted by international organizations, activists may have actively discouraged such framing at the local level because it subtly implies that circumcised women are "exotic others" (Gunning 1990–91; Kouba and Muasher 1985). This result may also indicate that elaborated frames are not necessarily more persuasive than restricted frames, when considered at the individual level.

Our next consideration was predicting which adherents would adopt particular explanations. Snow and Benford note that the potency of a frame depends on its relevance to the targeted population (1992). Because women in our sample who are circumcised must consciously reject a locally institutionalized practice, we predicted that they would be more likely to articulate a specific explanation for their opposition and that the frames of international actors would be more likely to resonate with them. Snow and Benford also suggest that a frame is more likely to "strike a responsive chord [if] it rings true with extant beliefs" (1992, 140). Being circumcised may indicate adherence to a non-Western belief system, which may make women suspicious of Western notions of human rights (Hoeschen 1999). Women who are embedded within such an alternative belief system may be particularly likely to find the restricted medical frame appealing because it allows them to oppose the practice of FGC without criticizing other aspects of their culture, such as overall gender roles. Further, in the case of FGC, circumcised women are the targeted population; the international organizations want to convince these women to not circumcise their daughters. For all these reasons, we expected circumcised women to frame their opposition to FGC in terms very different from bystanders (i.e., women who have never experienced circumcision and who live in communities where the practice is very rare).

In descriptive statistics, we found that constitutive explanations alone were much less common among circumcised women than uncircumcised women. Women who were circumcised themselves but reject FGC have consciously reflected on whether the practice is valuable. The consciousness of the process for these women was reflected in their greater use of the international frames. As noted above, table 8.1 indicates that for uncircumcised women, the most salient explanation for opposing the continuation of FGC was a constitutive explanation (74 percent). Circumcised women, in contrast, were more likely to use articulated explanations rather than simply saying FGC was a bad tradition. While 36 percent of uncircumcised women said only that FGC is a bad tradition, only 13 percent of circumcised women used that definitional explanation.

With respect to the frames of international activists, for circumcised women, constitutive explanations and medical explanations were equally frequent. However, circumcised women were more likely to use a medical explanation (54 percent) than uncircumcised women (25 percent). This suggests that the medical frame was more powerful for women who have experienced circumcision themselves. The ungrouped explanations provide additional support for this conclusion. The more closely related to personal experience, the greater the differences across circumcised and uncircumcised women. Although only 19 percent of uncircumcised women mentioned medical complications as the basis for their opposition to FGC, 40 percent of circumcised women employed this explanation. Likewise, only 8 percent of uncircumcised women used pain as their justification for opposing FGC, but 24 percent of circumcised women did. Finally, although only 5 percent of uncircumcised women specifically noted that FGC reduced sexual satisfaction, 12 percent of circumcised women used this reasoning. One implication of these findings is that frame resonance may operate differently for bystanders than it does for targeted populations. Fundamentally, the frames of international activists were clearly important, but their usefulness varied according to the adherents' personal experience.

We then turned once again to hierarchical modeling techniques— this time to determine how women's personal situations and their regional and national environments influenced how they framed their opposition to FGC. The models considered the probability that a woman would use a medical, human rights, or "constitutive" explanation, respectively, to justify her opposition relative to the other two explanation categories.

Our results indicated that circumcised women were 42 percent less likely to give a constitutive explanation than another explanation and 22 percent more likely to give a human rights explanation. However, circumcised women were *169 percent* more likely to give a medical explanation than another explanation. This supports the reasoning that circumcised women are more likely to articulate a specific reason for their anti-FGC attitude because they are consciously rejecting a local norm. The finding also suggests, as predicted, that personal experience (expressed through health concerns) becomes a particularly important instrumental rationale for opposition by circumcised women. Finally, it suggests that women belonging to cultures where FGC has traditionally been practiced are less amenable to a human rights discourse than a medical discourse.

Building on the analysis in the last chapter, exposure to the ideas of the international system in general and Western culture in particular is also likely to influence a woman's elaboration of why she opposes FGC. A woman in contact with Western script carriers is more likely to hear activist frames firsthand, and she is also more likely to relate to them and understand them when she does hear them. In addition, individuals outside the scope of the modern international system may experience the international norm in only a very remote, "ripple effect" manner. These individuals may be able to articulate the international principle but not specific justifications for it. For these reasons, we had predicted that exposure to the international system and Western culture (the direct or indirect source of most international norms) would be key factors in individuals' framing of their opposition to FGC.

The results of the analysis supported this prediction. Both college attendance and exposure to health care professionals increased the probability of a woman explaining her opposition to FGC with a medical or human rights explanation. All else being equal, attending college increased the likelihood of giving a medical explanation by 151 percent and of giving a human rights explanation by 103 percent. Encounters with health care professionals increased the probability of giving a medical explanation by 75 percent and a human rights explanation by 101 percent. In sum, exposure to Western culture through college and health care professionals notably increased the probability of both medical and human rights explanations for women opposing FGC.

As noted in the last chapter, two important indicators of independence for a woman are whether she lives in an urban area and whether she works outside the home. Informal social control tends to be weaker in urban areas, compared with rural areas, because in urban areas individuals tend to exist more independently and rely less on their kin for their future well-being. Working outside of the home may also remove women from local traditional networks and weaken informal social controls. Adherents who are less constrained by informal social control may be more able to openly discuss FGC, which is typically a taboo topic. For example, women who work outside the home have a greater chance of being exposed to individuals who are willing to discuss FGC and who articulate justifications for opposing the practice. Personal experiences, such as medical complications, are likely to be particularly important in such one-to-one interactions facilitated by women's independence. Thus, we had expected the medical frame to resonate with women who are relatively independent of traditional networks.

These predictions were borne out. Living in an urban area and working outside the home for pay significantly decreased the probability of giving a constitutive explanation for opposing FGC. The probability of a constitutive explanation decreased 22 percent for women who worked outside the home and 21 percent for women who lived in an urban area. Likewise, the probability of a medical explanation increased 15 percent for women who worked outside the home and 25 percent for women who lived in an urban area. Thus, independence appeared to make women particularly more likely to invoke a medical explanation for opposing the continuation of FGC.

Turning next to the regional context, we had surmised that women raised in a community where FGC is supported would be more likely to articulate a precise explanation for their opposition to the practice and to emphasize medicine in their explanation. As with women who have themselves experienced FGC, women in these regions will have consciously reflected on their opposition to the practice. They will find medical explanations for their opposition particularly salient because those explanations are not seen as a threat to their culture generally. In fact, the data indicated that living in a region that exhibits a high level of cultural support for FGC increases the likelihood of a medical explanation by 144 percent.

Modernization theory focuses specifically on the structural sources of local attitudes and is therefore also relevant to our analysis. However, the analysis described here uncovered little support for the idea, derived from Bell's modernization thesis, that the more developed a region (in terms of industrialism and literacy), the less likely a woman would be to provide a constitutive explanation for opposing FGC.

With respect to country differences, compared to women in Sudan, women in all other countries are more likely to give a human rights explanation for opposing FGC. The effect was quite marked—women in the other four countries are approximately three to four times more likely than women in Sudan to give a human rights explanation. This is powerful evidence that international frames *do* matter. Sudan was the only country in which the sample was drawn prior to the publication of the 1995 joint statement. As noted above, the joint statement suggested a shift in the framing strategies of international actors from a medical frame to a human rights frame. Our analysis demonstrated that women in all countries sampled after the strategy shift were more likely to express their opposition by using the human rights frame.

In sum, we had hypothesized that medical frames would be particularly prominent for circumcised women and that women with the closest links to Western culture and greater independence from local traditional networks would be more likely to use activist frames than women with less exposure to Western values. In terms of regional context, we had also hypothesized that cultural support for FGC and greater levels of development would lead opponents of the practice to be more articulate in their explanations and to rely more on scientific (i.e., medical) explanations for their opposition. Our analysis of the Demographic and Health Survey data supported these hypotheses.

Cultural Conflict and Framing

The effect of local context on rationale selection has important implications for the relationship between activist frames and the individual cognitions of a targeted population. Even among adherents, many individuals, when asked why they opposed FGC, did not articulate *any* of the frames promoted by international activists. Many individuals provided only a constitutive explanation for their position—that is, the practice is bad by definition. As frame theorists predict, experience plays an important role in this regard. Circumcised women were more likely than uncircumcised women to articulate a specific rather than a constitutive explanation for their adherence to the anti-FGC platform. Circumcised women were also particularly likely to link to the personally salient medical frame promoted by international activists. Our results clearly supported the theorized connection between experience and frame resonance. Our findings also suggested, however, that the need for frame resonance as a precondition for adherence may be contingent on experience. In other words, the explicit cognitive process of frame resonance may be less important for creating adherents out of bystanders than out of targeted populations.

A related point calls attention to "adherents" who exist prior to mobilization. Presumably, for most issues there are a significant number of individuals whose agreement with a social movement's goals predates the social movement. Although frame resonance may be irrelevant for these individuals, these individuals are not unimportant to a social movement's success. In an insightful article on infibulation, Mackie uses a convention account to explain how changes in behavior may follow the creation of a "critical mass" of opinions supporting change (1996). The implication is that regardless of whether they link into the frames of activists, all adherents are critical for social movement success. Acknowledging a looser connection between activist frames, individual frame resonance, and movement success allows for enhanced theorizing about when social movements are successful.

Another contribution is to identify individuals who are most likely to adopt the frames of international activists. In the last chapter, I related our finding that exposure to the international system and independence from traditional networks makes individuals more likely to deviate from traditional social practices. Here, the same factors that make women more likely to abandon a social tradition also make women more likely to use international activist frameworks to explain their opposition to that tradition. Women who were exposed to Western culture and were relatively independent of local networks were the most likely to link into the frames of international activists.

In an interesting twist, however, circumcised women were the adherents *most* likely to tap into the international discourse. This contrasts with the finding that circumcised women are the *least* likely to change their attitudes or behavior with respect to circumcision. Combining the findings, the overall pattern is that circumcised women are less likely than their uncircumcised counterparts to be persuaded by international activists, but if they are persuaded, they are particularly attuned to the frames of international activists. Further, a local cultural milieu supporting FGC makes women from that culture who oppose the practice more articulate in their reasoning.

The final contribution of the analysis described here is to provide support for the proposition that science, perhaps because of its perceived neutrality, is more persuasive than a broader, less specific discourse of human rights (see chapter 3). This finding is consistent with epistemic communities theory (Haas 1990). The finding is also relevant to frame theory's delineation of restricted and elaborated master frames. As their names imply, restricted frames are more specific and less open to multiple interpretations. Elaborated frames are more loosely defined. In the case of FGC, the medical frame is more restricted while the human rights frame is more elaborated. Frame theorists propose that elaborated frames foster more mobilization because of their flexibility, but our findings suggest a caveat. Although elaborated frames provide more flexibility, they appear to offer less explanatory power for movement adherents. This finding could be unique to the case of FGC, however, because personal experience and medical science are more closely tied for FGC than for some other issues.

NINE

Conclusion

At each level of analysis—international, national, and individual—global institutions framed reform against FGC. At each level of analysis, the structural location of groups and individuals influenced their enactment of institutionalized actions and beliefs. And at each level of analysis, institutionalized conflicts shaped change.

At the international level, human rights eventually took precedence, but the principle of national autonomy continued to shape reform efforts. Institutional conflict created spaces for reform and resistance. For example, the contradictions between institutionalized individualism and the institution of national autonomy led to "apolitical" medical intervention to reduce the incidence of FGC. This reframing of intervention technically preserved both individual rights and national sovereignty. Later, a similar result ensued when an individual rights discourse "won out" over the idea of family autonomy. Both nation and family were somewhat reconstituted to fit the new compromises. This suggests that institutions more closely linked to individualism take precedence in generating change.

Not all international actors played an equal role in reform. Generally, the more tightly an organization was linked to individualistic principles, the faster it signed on to reform efforts. The different structural positions of states, international governmental organizations (IGOs), and nongovernmental organizations (NGOs) are linked but unique, and their uniqueness shapes each entity's priorities and strategies of action. All of these organizations are constituted by and immersed in global institutions. This forces the three types of international actors to take each other seriously. Nevertheless, NGOs tended to be the staunchest supporters of the principle of gender equality in the realm of FGC. Without NGO intervention, policies devised through the collaboration of states and IGOs might well have remained decoupled indefinitely. Less predictable and often more coercive, NGOs make radical proposals for change and thus raise the baseline for the range of action nation-states should take. In contrast, states often take a more "realistic" and gradualist approach to international norms, which can disguise reluctance or inability to implement change. The interplay of these major actors in the international arena forces a tighter coupling between ideal and action over time.

At the national level, representative democracy sometimes conflicted with the notion of universal human rights. This both fueled decoupling and created an implicit "hierarchy" of values. FGC illustrated how the policies of separate nation-states are not always the outcome of local political processes but may well be one component of an international process.

Viewing national legislation as part of an international process has important implications for explaining both national and international action. At the national level, reform is often a top-down process. For example, although 97 percent of the women in Egypt are circumcised, the Egyptian health minister has banned the practice and the wife of the Egyptian president is spearheading an effort to eradicate FGC. This suggests that national laws are developed to change rather than reflect local attitudes. Further, despite the consistency of legalization across countries, we did find important West-South variation in national strategies. In some African countries, local communities figured into the process—but, contrary to democratic principles, as something to be worked around. These countries tended to avoid formal legislation that would involve representative bodies; they opted for more bureaucratic policies. Western countries, in contrast, adopted formal laws. This finding suggests that there should be an extension of institutional theory that incorporates variation in the manifestation of international ideals in different settings (cf. Grattet, Jenness, and Curry 1996). Whether there is a consistent disjuncture between bureaucratic policies and local culture in African countries is an important question.

Viewing lawmaking as an international rather than national process has important consequences. One implication is that the contradiction among international institutions can put a check on the progression of any particular ideal. Specifically, in the contest between democratic representation and human rights in the FGC realm, the human rights ideal dominates. States adopt laws that prohibit the practice even when the laws do not reflect the desires of their local constituencies. Nevertheless, the ideal of democratic representation continues to have an important effect on the process. This is evident in the deference that IGOs give to the sovereign authority of nation-states. These organizations use primarily assimilative strategies: including African nations in the policymaking process, having Western countries "model" appropriate national action, and promoting local anti-FGC mobilization within African countries. Respect for sovereign autonomy influences international actors to adopt less intrusive, assimilative reform policies rather than more directly instrumental, coercive policies. In contrast, actors in the international system who exist apart from the sovereignty system (NGOs, media, etc.) or who represent hegemonic authority (the United States, France) tend to be considerably less deferential to sovereign authority. This suggests that there may be infinite possibilities for social development at the point where "universal" principles contradict, so that the development of any ideal is somewhat constrained.

It also seems to be true that when institutions contradict each other, the one most closely linked to individualism predominates. This may indicate that a new conception of power, one that recognizes the empowering possibilities of the global narratives, is needed. Power and exploitation exist on many levels in the world. While some link FGC to patriarchal family, religion, and political structures that exploit women, others link Western pressures regarding FGC to postcolonial imperialism. Regardless, although Western pressure forced Southern nation-states to adopt anti-FGC policies, many would characterize international mobilization against FGC as *empowering local women* who did not want to undergo the practice (see a similar example from Merry [1995] on wife beating). Thus, whether the international system stripped away power or provided power is an open question. In fact, it appears to have done both. Thus, theorizing power is as important in research focusing on global narratives as in research focusing on agency and particular individuals.

The implications of institutional contradictions were different within different countries (e.g., Egypt, Tanzania, and the United States). Policies' relevance to local populations and a country's standing within the international community combined to fuel resistance to national reform. The country in which an anti-FGC policy had the most relevance—Egypt—also faced the most conflict about FGC.

The most concrete institutional conflict occurred at the individual level. Here, even among individuals who agreed with the goal of international actors, explanations for an anti-FGC position tended to avoid the invocation of human rights ideals. At the individual level, unique local attributes, such as a commitment to Islam, provided a specific alternative meaning system to the one carried by the international system. Religious background had an important impact on attitudes toward FGC and decisions to circumcise daughters. In addition, religion mediated the effects of other variables, such as exposure to Western principles.

The theme of predictable variation in the effect of institutions was illustrated in the way individuals framed their opposition to FGC. The social context greatly influenced the explanations women gave. Although international organizations emphasize human rights as their basis for opposing FGC, in areas where FGC is institutionalized, women were more likely to articulate a medical explanation for their opposition to the practice. Because a medical discourse is perceived as less relevant to local culture in general, it is less threatening than a human rights discourse. This demonstrated that where one stands in relation to institutionalized principles determines whether and how those principles will be deployed.

Global institutions such as national sovereignty did not disappear, despite international intervention. Rather, the interrelationship between institutions changed radically over several decades. As it expands, rights discourse tends to undercut other institutionalized arrangements. In the case of FGC, the nation-state and the family have been particularly affected. Rationalism and individualism tend to win out over these more concrete structural arrangements. This causes new tensions, which are likely to promote additional changes in the future. For example, the family is still viewed as the primary source of local cultural transmission, but now it is also defined as a site of repression for women and children. Perhaps in the future, the family will be absorbed within the global institutional arrangement and be subject to the same processes of isomorphism that nation-states currently experience.

Being constituted by the global system does not spell the demise of an organization. Nation-states are not likely to disappear anytime soon because they move the projects of modernity and individualism forward. Rather than disappearing, organizations constituted by and within global institutions lose autonomy and become rather homogenized repositories of institution principles. FGC and other issues capturing the attention of international actors today certainly suggest that the family may be the current site for expanding universal individualism.

Although this book is important as an analysis of the critically controversial issue of FGC, it has broader implications as well. By (1) addressing the complex relationships between international actors, nation-states, and individuals; (2) explaining the increasing involvement of international actors in local cultural practices; and (3) theorizing the substance and interaction of institutions, I hope I have offered insights into many other types of cultural conflict in the international system.

NOTES

. . . .

Preface

1. Erin Moriarty, "Not Tonight Dear: Low Sex Drive in Women Can Be Treated with Hormone Therapy If Properly Diagnosed," CBS News Transcripts, *48 Hours,* Burrelle's Information Services, 5 April 2001.

ONE Introduction

1. Judy Mann, "When Journalists Witness Atrocities," *Washington Post,* 23 September 1994, E3.

2. See, e.g., Nabil Meghalli, "Circumcision Persists as Insult and Injury to Femininity," *Deutsche Presse-Agentur,* 12 September 1994; Shyam Bhatia, "The Cut That Tore a Veil of Tears," *Observer,* 9 October 1994, 22; Mann, "When Journalists Witness Atrocities," E3.

3. "Egyptian Producer Held over CNN Circumcision Film," *Reuters World Service,* 12 September 1994.

4. "Police Free Egyptian TV Producer," *Reuters World Service,* 12 September 1994; "Government Prepares Law Banning Female Circumcision, *Agence France Presse,* 26 September 1994.

5. "New Law Bans Adoption, but Not Female Circumcision in Egypt," *Agence France Presse,* 24 February 1996 (reporting on October 1994 *fatwa*).

6. Note use of alternative abbreviation, meaning "female genital mutilation." Future quotations also preserve author's original terminology.

7. Joery Fischer, "CNN Video Triggers Debate on Female Circumcision," *Deutsche Presse-Agentur,* 26 October 1994.

8. "Egypt Says Female Circumcision in Decline," *Reuters World Service,* 4 April 1995.

9. Mona Eltahawy, "Violence against Women Comes out of Shadows," *Reuters World Service,* 23 May 1995.

10. "Imam of Al-Azhar Goes on Trial for Urging Female Circumcision," *Agence France Presse*, 6 May 1995.

11. Sara Gauch, "Modern Egypt Says Ancient Rite Is Wrong," *Chicago Tribune*, 10 September 1995, 1; Judy Mann, "A Welcome Reversal," *Washington Post*, 27 December 1995, F13.

12. Gauch, "Modern Egypt," 1.

13. See Lancaster 1996.

14. Dezalay and Garth (1996) begin to parse out this process by examining the formation of international business arbitration. Although international arbitration involves individuals, what is taken for granted on a day-to-day basis is likely to be very different for those involved in high finance and those just struggling to survive. Specifically, while international arbitration operates largely "above" national governments, anti-FGC activists deal with individuals as they are immersed in their local milieu.

15. Culture is global (Waters 1995; Said 1993) and local (Mohanty 1991; Narayan 1997; Funder 1993; Shweder et al. 1997; Simms 1993).

16. A related American domestic example is the case of affirmative action, where opponents of affirmative action could not argue against equal employment opportunity. See Pedriana and Stryker 1997.

TWO Understanding Female Genital Cutting

1. Asma Abdel Halim's name is given as Asma Mohammed A'Haleem in A'Haleem 1992.

2. Judith Fox, *Sacramento Bee*, 17 May 1996, B7.

3. Janice Boddy's (1991) assessment that although female researchers and their informants share a common biology, they do not share a common gender may be apt.

4. I learned this in conversations with Colman Titus and Fortunata Songora.

5. Recent case studies, however, suggest that fathers are beginning to take an active role in protecting their daughters from the practice (Kassindja and Bashir 1998).

6. Lucas Maseke, "Genital Mutilators Threaten to Resume Business," *The Guardian* (Dar Es Salaam, Tanzania), 17 April 2001.

7. The World Health Organization Web site has an Islamic expert suggesting that there are actually three possible *hadith* that apply to FGC (al-Awwa 2002). Al-Awwa argues that none are authentically linked to Mohammed, but even if they were, they do not actually require FGC.

8. The timing coincides with the first publication of Kenyatta's book.

THREE The Evolution of Debates over Female Genital Cutting

1. Pedriana and Stryker (1997) aptly note that this is not a feedback effect but a "feed forward" aspect of reform movements.

2. As Wendy Nelson Espeland notes, when an outcome takes on particular importance, whether that outcome is reached becomes the basis for determining the legitimacy of the process (1998, 225). For feminists, sovereign autonomy *could not* be legitimate because it allowed FGC to continue.

3. This is consistent with Anthony Giddens' characterization of modernization as disembedding local knowledge with abstract, expert systems such as medical science (1991, 17–23).

4. The current structure of the opposition to FGC suggests the presence of both an "epistemic community" (Haas 1990) and a "transnational advocacy network" (Keck and Sikkink 1998). In reality, epistemic communities and transnational advocacy networks overlap, but they can be distinguished conceptually by the way they frame the issue. By definition, an epistemic community focuses more on medical science, while a transnational advocacy network focuses more on the principle of human rights (Keck and Sikkink 1998, 30); compare Peter Haas, "Introduction: Epistemic Communities and International Policy Coordination," (1992).

5. Special thanks to Dongxiao Liu, who drafted much of this description of CEDAW and its history for a coauthored article that we currently have under review (Boyle and Liu 2002).

6. "States parties" is the formal term for states that have ratified an international treaty.

7. With respect to women, the rhetoric of the international system focuses on gender equality and women as citizens, with a goal of closing the gap between the reality of gender inequality and the ideal of equality (Bunch 1990, 174–75).

8. Some suggest that the ever-expanding conception of rights, and global intervention on their behalf, will force a re-imagining of the nation-state. See, e.g., Waters 1995.

FOUR International Mobilization

1. Asma Abdel Halim, Office of Women in Development, Bureau for Global Programs, Field Support and Research, U.S. Agency for International Development, letter to author, 16 July 1998.

2. My definition of NGOs does not include transnational corporations and religious institutions, or organizations controlled by these entities.

3. For a discussion of feminism from the perspective of third-world women, see Mohanty 1991; see also Gunning 1990–91.

4. See also Walker and Parmar 1993.

5. Soraya Mire, "A Call to End the Tradition of Genital Mutilation," *Chicago Tribune,* 18 July 1993.

6. "Female Genital Mutilation Persists in 28 African Countries," *Xinhua News Agency,* 26 June 1994.

7. Sara Gauch, "Modern Egypt Says Ancient Rite Is Wrong," *Chicago Tribune,* 10 September 1995, 1.

8. "American TV Crew Questioned on Film on Female Circumcision," *Deutsche Presse-Agentur,* 12 September 1994.

9. See, e.g., Nabil Meghalli, "Circumcision Persists as Insult and Injury to Femininity," *Deutsche Presse-Agentur,* 12 September 1994; Shyam Bhatia, "The Cut That Tore a Veil of Tears," *Observer,* 9 October 1994, 22; Judy Mann, "When Journalists Witness Atrocities," *Washington Post,* 23 September 1994, E3.

10. Dana Micucci, "What Do We Want? Equality. And When Do We Want It? Now," *Chicago Tribune,* 23 March 1997, 1.

11. Gauch, "Modern Egypt," 1; Judy Mann, "A Welcome Reversal," *Washington Post,* 27 December 1995, F13.

12. Mona Eltahawy, "Violence against Women Comes out of Shadows," *Reuters World Service,* 23 May 1995; "Imam of Al-Azhar Goes on Trial for Urging Female Circumcision," *Agence France Presse,* 6 May 1995.

13. For a discussion of how to make this law effective in Africa, see Sussman 1998.

FIVE The Diffusion of National Policies
against Female Genital Cutting

1. Sovereignty to some extent entails cultural autonomy; that is, states are expected to guard the cultural autonomy of their people, but the reverse is not necessarily true. Cultural autonomy is more linked to the notion of the right of national self-determination, which is held to apply even to people who do not have their own sovereign states, and it applies to people of different cultures living in one state.

2. Most of these countries have local organizations that oppose the practice.

3. For example, other countries with internal opposition to laws have experienced similar outcomes. In Chad, the government is cooperating with nongovernmental organizations (NGOs) to eliminate FGC through public awareness campaigns and seminars. A transitional government passed a law

making FGC punishable as an assault in 1995, and the law was signed by Chad's president. In Côte D'Ivoire, the president of the NGO l'Association Ivoirienne pour la Défense des Droits des Femmes has enlisted the support of the country's president in the campaign against FGC, and the National Minister of Communications has been an active participant and speaker at seminars. The Ministry of Family and Women's Affairs in Côte D'Ivoire has launched a campaign against the practice, and the government passed a law banning the practice in December 1998.

4. This excludes Liberia, where civil war disrupted village life to such an extent that the practice has been largely discontinued without active state intervention.

5. There was a rapid increase in immigration between 1990 and 1994 because of a change in immigration policy.

SIX Variation in the Meanings of National Policies

1. For more on the importance of power in diffusion processes, see also Dobbin and Dowd 2000.

2. "Barber Arrested after CNN Films Female Circumcision," *Agence France Presse,* 12 September 1994.

3. This is probably also related to Tanzania's lack of wealth; international organizations fund most of these studies and reports.

4. Joan Beck, "Stop the Mutilation of African Girls," *Denver Post,* 18 September 1994, E-04.

5. Abe M. Rosenthal, "On My Mind: Fighting Female Mutilation," *New York Times,* 12 April 1995, A31.

6. Judy Mann, "When Journalists Witness Atrocities," *Washington Post,* 27 December 1995, F13.

SEVEN Individual Response

1. The Demographic and Health Surveys or their precursors have been administered since 1974. The program is funded by the U.S. Agency for International Development. To demonstrate the quality of these data, we offer the example of the third Egyptian survey. The Demographic and Health Surveys used a multistage stratified sampling design in Egypt, and the response rate exceeded 98 percent for women. In addition, the sampling error was less than 2 percent for all representative variables (see El-Zanaty et al. 1996, appendices B and C). There is a great deal of confidence in the data.

2. Surveys were completed in the Central African Republic in 1994, in

Egypt in 1995, in Kenya in 1998, in Mali in 1995, in Niger in 1998, and in Sudan in 1989.

3. Data considerations were important in selecting the five countries. FGC occurs in each of the five countries, and recent Demographic and Health Surveys asked women about their attitudes and behavior with respect to FGC in each of the countries. No other countries have the complete repertoire of information.

4. Some modernization theories make a distinction between percentage employed in industry and percentage employed in service jobs. The percentage in the service sector in our regions was so low that this was not a useful distinction for our analysis.

5. Our reasoning here is that regional percent literate and regional percent with electricity affect individual's circumstances over and above individual education or electricity use.

EIGHT   Individual Frame Resonance

1. See also the debate over framing the issue in *Medical Anthropology Quarterly* (Gordon 1991; Ginsburg 1991).

2. The current structure of the opposition to FGC suggests the presence of both an "epistemic community" and a "transnational advocacy network." In reality, the two groups are well integrated, but they can be distinguished conceptually by the way they frame the issue. By definition, an epistemic community focuses more on medical science, while a transnational advocacy network focuses more on the principle of human rights (Keck and Sikkink 1998, 30).

3. Reluctance to use a human rights frame was in part the result of controversies at the Copenhagen conference of 1980, in which African women boycotted the panels of anti-FGC activists (Kouba and Muasher 1985).

4. For example, doctors at Harborview Medical Center in Seattle, Washington, indicated that they would be willing to conduct medically safe, small cuts (somewhat comparable to *sunna* circumcisions) on immigrant girls in their area. The vocal criticism from human rights activists (and nonimmigrant members of the local community) caused the program to be aborted (Coleman 1999).

5. We analyzed the data using hierarchical generalized linear models. For a more specific description of our method and results, see Boyle, Hoeschen, and Carbone (2002).

6. In Egypt and Mali, the surveys were administered to only women who were or had been married.

7. In Sudan, the categories "bad tradition" and "against my religion" were combined, so there were only eight possible categories.

8. One could argue that sexual satisfaction is as much about women's health as it is about women's rights (and self-expression). Thus, we ran the same analyses with the sexual satisfaction explanation paired with the medical explanation. The results did not change in any significant manner.

9. In composing the categories, we first looked for common themes. We then ran a correlation analysis to confirm the validity of the categories. On the assumption that women would not give responses they perceived as redundant, we expected and found that across categories, responses were negatively correlated with one another, and within categories, responses were not significantly correlated.

REFERENCES

A'Haleem, Asma Mohammed. 1992. "Claiming Our Bodies and Our Rights: Exploring Female Circumcision as an Act of Violence in Africa." In *Freedom from Violence: Women's Strategies from around the World,* ed. Margaret Schuler, 141–56. New York: United Nations Development Fund for Women.

Ahmadu, Fuambai. 2000. "Rites and Wrongs: An Insider/Outsider Reflects on Power and Excision." In *Female "Circumcision" in Africa: Culture, Controversy, and Change,* ed. Bettina Shell-Duncan and Ylva Hernlund, 283–312. Boulder, Colo.: Lynne Reinner Publishers.

al-Awwa, Muhammad Salim. 2002. "Female Circumcision: Neither a Sunna, nor a Sign of Respect." www.who.sci.eg/Publications/HealthEdReligion/CircumcisionEn/.

Anderson, Ellen. 1994. "Legislating Cultural Change: Female Genital Mutilation." *Hennepin Lawyer,* September–October: 16–19.

Asali, Abed, Naif Khamaysi, Yunis Aburabia, Simha Letzer, Buteina Halihal, Moshe Sadovsky, Benjamin Maoz, and R.H. Belmaker. 1995. "Ritual Female Genital Surgery Among Bedouin in Israel." *Archives of Sexual Behavior* 24: 571–75.

Assaad, Marie Bassilli. 1980. "Female Circumcision in Egypt: Social Implications, Current Research, and Prospects for Change." *Studies in Family Planning* 11: 3–16.

Atoki, Morayo. 1995. "Should Female Circumcision Continue to Be Banned?" *Feminist Legal Studies* 3, no. 2: 223–35.

Babatunde, Emmanuel. 1998. *Women's Rights versus Women's Rites: A Study of Circumcision among the Ketu Yoruba of South Western Nigeria.* Trenton, N.J.: Africa World Press.

Bahar, Saba. 1996. "Human Rights Are Women's Rights: Amnesty International and the Family." *Hypatia* 11: 105–34.

Barker-Benfield, Graham J. 1975. "Sexual Surgery in Late Nineteenth-Century America." *International Journal of Health Services* 5: 279–98.

————. 1976. "A Historical Perspective on Women's Health Care." *Women & Health* 1: 13–20.

Barnett, Michael N., and Martha Finnemore. 1999. "The Politics, Power, and Pathologies of International Organizations." *International Organization* 53: 699–732.

Barrett, Deborah, and David John Frank. 1999. "Population Control for National Development: From World Discourse to National Policies." In *Constructing World Culture: International Nongovernmental Organizations since 1875,* ed. John Boli and George M. Thomas, 198–221. Stanford, Calif.: Stanford University Press.

Bashir, Layli Miller. 1996. "Female Genital Mutilation in the United States: An Examination of Criminal and Asylum Law." *Journal of Gender and the Law* 4: 415–54.

Bell, Daniel. 1973. *The Coming of Post-Industrial Society.* New York: Basic Books.

————. 1976. *The Cultural Contradictions of Capitalism.* New York: Basic Books.

Berkovitch, Nitza. 1999a. "The Emergence and Transformation of the International Women's Movement." In *Constructing World Culture: International Nongovernmental Organizations since 1875,* ed. John Boli and George M. Thomas, 100–26. Stanford, Calif.: Stanford University Press.

————. 1999b. *From Motherhood to Citizenship: Women's Rights and International Organizations.* Baltimore, Md.: Johns Hopkins University Press.

Berkovitch, Nitza, and Karen Bradley. 1999. "The Globalization of Women's Status: Consensus/Dissensus in the World Polity." *Sociological Perspectives* 42: 481–98.

Bibbings, Lois. 1995. "Female Circumcision: Mutilation or Modification?" In *Law and Body Politics: Regulating the Female Body,* ed. Jo Bridgeman and Susan Millns, 151–70. Brookfield, Vt.: Dartmouth Publishing Company.

Bielefeldt, Heiner. 1995. "Muslim Voices in the Human Rights Debate." *Human Rights Quarterly* 17: 587–617.

Black, J.A., and G.D. Debelle. 1995. "Female Genital Mutilation in Britain," *British Medical Journal* 310: 1590–92.

Boddy, Janice. 1982. "Womb as Oasis: The Symbolic Context of Pharaonic Circumcision in Rural Northern Sudan." *American Ethnologist* 9: 682–98.

————. 1989. *Wombs and Alien Spirits: Women, Men, and the Zar Cult in Northern Sudan.* Madison, Wisc.: University of Wisconsin Press.

————. 1991. "Body Politics: Continuing the Anti-Circumcision Crusade." *Medical Anthropology Quarterly* 5: 15–17.

Boli, John. 1999. "Conclusion: World Authority Structures and Legitimations." In *Constructing World Culture: International Nongovernmental Organi-*

zations since 1875, ed. John Boli and George M. Thomas, 267–302. Stanford, Calif.: Stanford University Press.

Boli, John, and George M. Thomas. 1997. World Culture in the World Polity: A Century of International Non-Governmental Organization. *American Sociological Review* 62: 171–90.

Boli, John, and George M. Thomas. 1999a. *Constructing World Culture: International Nongovernmental Organizations since 1875.* Stanford, Calif.: Stanford University Press, 1999.

———. "Introduction." 1999b. In *Constructing World Culture: International Nongovernmental Organizations since 1875,* ed. John Boli and George M. Thomas, 1–12. Stanford, Calif.: Stanford University Press.

Boulware-Miller, Kay. 1985. "Female Circumcision: Challenges to the Practice as a Human Rights Violation." *Harvard Women's Law Journal* 8: 155–77.

Boyle, Elizabeth Heger. 1998. "Political Frames and Legal Activity: The Case of Nuclear Power in Four Countries." *Law & Society Review* 32: 141–74.

Boyle, Elizabeth Heger, and Andrea Hoeschen. 2001. "Theorizing the Form of Media Coverage over Time." *The Sociological Quarterly* 42: 511–27.

Boyle, Elizabeth Heger, Kristin Carbone, and Andrea Hoeschen. 2002. "International Master Frames and African Women's Explanations for Opposing Female Genital Cutting." Paper presented at the Annual Meetings of the American Sociological Association, August 16, 2002, Chicago, Ill.

Boyle, Elizabeth Heger, and Dongxiao Liu. 2002. "Free to Criticize? Sovereignty, Accountability, and the International Reform Strategies of States, IGOs, and NGOs." Work in progress.

Boyle, Elizabeth Heger, Barbara McMorris, and Mayra Gómez. 2002. "Local Conformity to International Norms: The Case of Female Genital Cutting." *International Sociology* 17: 5–33.

Boyle, Elizabeth Heger, and John W. Meyer. 1998. "Modern Law as a Secularized and Global Model: Implications for the Sociology of Law." *Soziale Welt* 49: 213–32.

Boyle, Elizabeth Heger, and Sharon Preves. 2000. "National Legislating as an International Process: The Case of Anti-Female-Genital-Cutting Laws." *Law & Society Review* 34: 401–32.

Boyle, Elizabeth Heger, Fortunata Songora, and Gail Foss. 2001. "International Discourse and Local Politics: Anti-Female-Genital-Cutting Laws in Egypt, Tanzania, and the United States." *Social Problems* 48: 524–44.

Brennan, Katherine. 1989. "The Influence of Cultural Relativism on International Human Rights Law: Female Circumcision as a Case Study." *Law and Inequality* 7: 367–98.

Brinton, Mary C., and Victor Nee. 1998. *The New Institutionalism in Sociology.* New York: Russell Sage Foundation.

Brown, Nathan. 1995. "Law and Imperialism: Egypt in Comparative Perspective." *Law & Society Review* 29: 103–22.

Bunch, Charlotte. 1990. "Women's Rights as Human Rights: Toward a Revision of Human Rights." *Human Rights Quarterly* 12: 486–98.

California State Senate. 1997. "The California Bill Text Statenet: California 1995–96 Regular Session Assembly Bill 2125." www.sen.ca.gov/

Carr, Dara. 1997. *Female Genital Cutting: Findings from the Demographic and Health Surveys Program.* Calverton, Md.: Macro International.

Center for Reproductive Law and Policy and International Federation of Women Lawyers. 1997. *Women of the World: Laws and Policies Affecting Their Reproductive Health.* New York, NY.

Chabbott, Colette. 1999. "Population Control for National Development: From World Discourse to National Policies." In *Constructing World Culture: International Nongovernmental Organizations since 1875,* ed. John Boli and George M. Thomas, 222–48. Stanford, Calif.: Stanford University Press.

Charlesworth, Hillary. 1995. "Human Rights as Men's Rights." In *Women's Rights, Human Rights: International Feminist Perspectives,* ed. Julie Peters and Andrea Wolper, 103–13. New York: Routledge.

Cheng, P., and About, A. 1999. *Female Genital Mutilation (FGM): The Legal Point of View.* Paper presented at the National Conference on Female Genital Mutilation, Dodoma, Tanzania.

Coleman, Doriane Lambelet. 1998. "Individualizing Justice through Multiculturalism: The Liberal's Dilemma." *Columbia Law Review* 96: 1093–167.

———. 1999. "The Seattle Compromise: Multicultural Sensitivity and Americanization." *Duke Law Journal* 47: 717–84.

Congressional Record. 1995a. "Introduction of Legislation to Prevent Female Genital Mutilation and the Dangers of the National Security Revitalization Act." 14 February.

———. 1995b. "Statements on Introduced Bills and Joint Resolutions—The Federal Prohibition of Female Genital Mutilation Act of 1995." 13 July.

———. 1995c. "Legislation Making FGM Illegal." 19 October.

———. 1996. "Immigration Control Responsibility Act of 1996." 29 April.

Cook, Rebecca J., ed. 1994. *Human Rights of Women: National and International Perspectives.* Philadelphia: University of Pennsylvania Press.

Coomaraswamy, Radhika. 1999. "Reinventing International Law: Women's Rights as Human Rights in the International Community." In *Debating Human Rights: Critical Essays from the United States and Asia,* ed. Peter Van Ness, 167–83. London: Routledge.

Dallmeyer, Dorinda G., ed. 1993. *Reconceiving Reality: Women and International Law.* Studies in Transnational Legal Policy No. 25. Washington, D.C.: American Society of International Law.

Daly, Mary. 1978. *Gyn/Ecology: The Metaethics of Radical Feminism.* Boston: Beacon Press.

Dawit, Seble, and Salem Mekuria. 1993. "The West Just Doesn't Get It." *New York Times,* 7 December: A33.

Dezalay, Yves, and Bryant G. Garth. 1996. *Dealing in Virtue: International Commercial Arbitration and the Construction of a Transnational Legal Order.* Chicago: University of Chicago Press.

Dillon, Susan A. 2000. "Healing the Sacred Yoni in the Land of Isis: Female Genital Mutilation Is Banned (Again) in Egypt." *Houston Journal of International Law* 22: 289–326.

DiMaggio, Paul, and Walter Powell. 1983. "The Iron Cage Revisited: Institutional Isomorphism and Collective Rationality in Organizational Fields." *American Sociological Review* 48: 147–60.

DiMaggio, Paul, and Walter Powell, eds. 1991. *The New Institutionalism in Organizational Analysis.* Chicago: University of Chicago Press.

Dobbin, Frank, and Timothy J. Dowd. 2000. "The Market That Antitrust Built: Public Policy, Private Coercion, and Railroad Acquisitions, 1825–1922," *American Sociological Review* 65: 631–57.

Dorkenoo, Efua. 1995. *Cutting the Rose: Female Genital Mutilation, the Practice and Its Prevention.* London: Minority Rights Publications.

Dugger, Celia W. 1996. "New Law Bans Genital Cutting in United States: Violators Could Face Five Years in Prison." *New York Times,* 12 October: 1A.

Dullea, Georgia. 1980. "Female Circumcision a Topic at UN Parley." *New York Times,* 18 July: B4.

Edelman, Lauren, Christopher Uggen, and Howard Erlanger. 1999. "The Endogeneity of Legal Regulation: Grievance Procedures as Rational Myth." *American Journal of Sociology* 105: 406–54.

Edelman, Murray. 1964. *The Symbolic Uses of Politics.* Urbana: University of Illinois Press.

El Dareer, Asma. 1982. *Woman, Why Do You Weep?* Westport, Conn.: Lawrence Hill & Co.

El-Zanaty, Fatma, Enas M. Hussein, Gihan A. Shawky, Ann A. Way, and Sunita Kishor. 1996. *Egypt Demographic and Health Survey 1995.* Cairo, Egypt: National Population Council.

Enquête Démographique et de Santé du Mali. 1995–96. Bamako: Centre pour la Population et la Santé, Direction National de la Statistique et de l'Information.

Enquête Démographique et de Santé du Niger. 1998. Niamey: CARE International.

Equality Now. 1997. "Around the World: Canada." *Awaken* 1 (June): 4.

Espeland, Wendy Nelson. 1998. *The Struggle for Water: Politics, Rationality, and Identity in the American Southwest.* Chicago: University of Chicago Press.

Etienne, Margareth. 1995. "Addressing Gender-Based Violence in an International Context." *Harvard Women's Law Journal* 18: 139–70.

Etzioni, Amatai. 2000. "Social Norms: Internalization, Persuasion, and History." *Law & Society Review* 34: 157–78.

Ezzat, Dina. 1994. "In the Shadow of a Man: Social Forces and Women's Rights in Egypt." In *Private Decisions, Public Debate: Women, Reproduction & Population,* ed. Judith Mirsky, 163–85. London: Panos.

Fadiman, Anne. 1997. *The Spirit Catches You and You Fall Down: A Hmong Child, Her American Doctors, and the Collision of Two Cultures.* New York: Farrar, Straus, and Giroux.

Ferguson, James. 1994. *The Anti-Politics Machine: "Development," Depoliticization, and Bureaucratic Power in Lesotho.* Minneapolis: University of Minnesota Press.

Finnemore, Martha. 1996. *National Interests in International Society.* Ithaca, N.Y.: Cornell.

Franck, Thomas. 1990. *The Power of Legitimacy among Nations.* New York: Oxford.

Frank, David John, and Elizabeth McEneaney. 1999. "The Individualization of Society and the Liberalization of State Policies on Same-Sex Relations, 1984–1995." *Social Forces* 77: 911–43.

Frank, David John, Evan Schofer, and Ann Hironaka. 2000. "The Nation-State and the Environment over the Twentieth Century." *American Sociological Review* 65: 96–116.

Fraser, Arvonne. n.d. "Eliminating Discrimination against Women: From a Declaration to a Convention." Unpublished manuscript, Humphrey Institute of Public Affairs, University of Minnesota.

Friedland, Roger, and Robert Alford. 1991. "Bringing Society Back In: Symbols, Practices, and Institutional Contradictions." In *The New Institutionalism in Organizational Analysis,* ed. Walter Powell and Paul DiMaggio, 232–65. Chicago: University of Chicago Press.

Funder, Anne. 1993. "De Minimus Non Curat Lex: The Clitoris, Culture and the Law." *Transnational Law and Contemporary Problems* 3: 417–67.

Gaete, Rolando. 1991. "Postmodernism and Human Rights: Some Insidious Questions." *Law and Critique* 2: 149–70.

Geiger, Susan. 1997. *Tanu Women: Gender and Culture in the Making of Tangan-*

yikan Nationalism, 1955–1965. Social History of Africa Series. Portsmouth, N.H.: Heinemann.

Giddens, Anthony. 1991. *Modernity and Self-Identity: Self and Society in the Late Modern Age.* Stanford, Calif.: Stanford University Press.

———. 1992. *The Transformation of Intimacy: Sexuality, Love and Eroticism in Modern Societies.* Stanford, Calif.: Stanford University Press.

Ginsburg, Faye. 1991. "What Do Women Want? Feminist Anthropology Confronts Clitoridectomy." *Medical Anthropology Quarterly* 5: 17–19.

Gluckman, Max. 1955. *Custom and Conflict in Africa.* Oxford, U.K.: Blackwell.

Gómez, Mayra. 2001. *Towards a Sociological Understanding of Human Rights Abuse: The Intersection of International Pressure and Internal Politics.* Ph.D. diss., University of Minnesota.

Gordon, Daniel. 1991. "Female Circumcision and Genital Operations in Egypt and the Sudan: A Dilemma for Medical Anthropology." *Medical Anthropology Quarterly* 5: 3–14.

Grattet, Ryken, Valerie Jenness, and Theodore Curry. 1996. "The Homogenization and Differentiation of Hate Crime Law in the United States, 1978 to 1995: Innovation and Diffusion in the Criminalization of Bigotry." *American Sociological Review* 63: 286–307.

Griswold, Wendy. 1994. *Cultures and Societies in a Changing World.* Thousand Oaks, Calif.: Pine Forge Press.

Gruenbaum, Ellen. 1991. "The Islamic Movement, Development, and Health Education." *Social Science and Medicine* 33: 637–45.

———. 2001. *The Female Circumcision Controversy.* Philadelphia: University of Pennsylvania Press.

Gunning, Isabelle. 1990–91. "Arrogant Perception, World-Travelling and Multicultural Feminism: The Case of Female Genital Surgeries." *Columbia Human Rights Law Review* 23: 189–248.

———. 1999. "Global Feminism at the Local Level: Criminal and Asylum Laws Regarding Female Genital Surgeries." *Journal of Gender, Race and Justice* 3: 45–62.

Gusfield, Joseph R. 1986. *Symbolic Crusade: Status Politics and the American Temperance Movement.* 2nd ed. Urbana: University of Illinois Press.

Haas, Peter. 1992. "Introduction: Epistemic Communities and International Policy Coordination." *International Organization* 46: 1–35.

Haas, Peter M. 1990. *Saving the Mediterranean: The Politics of International Environmental Cooperation, The Political Economy of International Change.* New York: Columbia University Press.

Herman, Edward S., and Robert McChesney. 1997. *The Global Media: The New Missionaries of Global Capitalism.* London: Cassell.

Hicks, Esther K. 1993. *Infibulation: Female Mutilation in Islamic Northern Africa.* New Brunswick, N.J.: Transaction.

Hoeschen, Andrea. 1999. "Epistemic Communities and the Creation of Consent." Master's thesis, University of Minnesota.

Hosken, Fran. 1979. *The Hosken Report—Genital and Sexual Mutilations of Females.* 2nd ed. Lexington, Mass.: Women's International Network News.

———. 1981. "Female Genital Mutilation in the World Today: A Global Review." *International Journal of Health Services* 11: 415–30.

Hughes, Karen. 1995. "The Criminalization of Female Genital Mutilation in the United States." *Journal of Law and Policy* 4: 321–70.

Ierodiaconou, Mary-Jane. 1995. "'Listen to Us!' Female Genital Mutilation, Feminism, and the Law in Australia." *Melbourne Law Review* 20: 562–87.

Information Please Almanacs. 1999. *Almanacs—World—Country.* www.info please.com.

Inglehart, Ronald, and Wayne E. Baker. 2000. "Modernization, Cultural Change, and the Persistence of Traditional Values." *American Sociological Review* 65: 19–51.

Inkeles, Alex. 1971. "Continuity and Change in the Interaction of the Personal and the Sociocultural Systems." In *Stability and Social Change,* ed. Bernard Barber and Alex Inkeles, 265–84. Boston: Little, Brown.

———. 1996. "Making Men Modern: On the Causes and Consequences of Individual Change in Six Developing Countries." In *Comparing Nations and Cultures: Readings in a Cross-Disciplinary Perspective,* ed. Alex Inkeles and Masamichi Sasaki, 571–85. Englewood Cliffs, N.J.: Prentice Hall.

———. 1998. *One World Emerging: Convergence and Divergence in Industrial Societies.* Boulder, Colo.: Westview Press.

Inkeles, Alex, and David Smith. 1974. *Becoming Modern: Individual Changes in Six Developing Societies.* Cambridge: Harvard University Press.

Jackson, Robert H., and Alan James. 1993. *States in a Changing World: A Contemporary Analysis.* Oxford: Clarendon Press.

James, Stanlie. 1998. "Shades of Othering: Reflections on Female Circumcision/Genital Mutilation." *Signs: Journal of Women in Culture and Society* 23: 1031–48.

James, Stephen A. 1994. "Reconciling International Human Rights and Cultural Relativism: The Case of Female Circumcision." *Bioethics* 8: 1–26.

Jepperson, Ronald. 1991. "Institutions, Institutional Effects, and Institutionalism." In *The New Institutionalism in Organizational Analysis,* ed. Walter W. Powell and Paul J. DiMaggio, 143–63. Chicago: University of Chicago Press.

Johnson, Michelle C. 2000. "Becoming a Muslim, Becoming a Person: Female 'Circumcision,' Religious Identity, and Personhood in Guinea-

Bissau." In *Female "Circumcision" in Africa: Culture, Controversy, and Change*, ed. Bettina Shell-Duncan and Ylva Hernlund, 215–33. Boulder, Colo.: Lynne Reinner.

Jones, Wanda K., Jack Smith, Barney Kieke Jr., and Lynne Wilcox. 1997. "Female Genital Mutilation/Female Circumcision." *Public Health Reports* 112: 369–77.

Kassindja, Fauziya, and Layli Miller Bashir. 1998. *Do They Hear You When You Cry?* New York: Delta.

Keck, Margaret, and Kathryn Sikkink. 1998. *Activists without Borders: Transnational Advocacy in International Politics.* Ithaca, N.Y.: Cornell.

Kenyatta, Jomo. [1938] 1978. *Facing Mount Kenya: The Tribal Life of the Gikuyu.* Reprint, New York: Vintage.

Kijo-Bisimba, Helen, Sharon Lee, and John Wallace. 1999. *Report on the Findings of Research into the Practice of Female Genital Mutilation in Tanzania.* Dar Es Salaam, Tanzania: Konrad Adeneur Foundation/Legal and Human Rights Center.

Knight, Jack, and Jean Ensminger. 1998. "Conflict over Changing Social Norms: Bargaining, Ideology, and Enforcement." In *The New Institutionalism in Sociology*, ed. Mary Brinton and Victor Nee, 105–26. New York: Russell Sage.

Kouba, Leonard J., and Judith Muasher. 1985. "Female Circumcision in Africa: An Overview." *African Studies Review* 28: 95–110.

Lancaster, John. 1995. "Top Islamic University Gains Influence in Cairo: Al Azhar Reflects Revival of Fundamentalism," *Washington Post*, April 11: A14.

———. 1996. "Egyptians Stand by Female Circumcision; Tradition Flouts, Foreign Pressures to Eliminate the Risky Practice." *Washington Post*, November 24: A33.

Lane, Sandra D., and Robert A. Rubinstein. 1996. "Judging the Other: Responding to Traditional Female Genital Surgeries." *Hastings Center Report* 26, no. 3: 31–40.

Leonard, Lori. 1996. "Female Circumcision in Southern Chad: Origins, Meaning, and Current Practice." *Social Science Medicine* 43: 255–63.

———. 2000. "'We Did It for Pleasure Only': Hearing Alternative Tales of Female Circumcision." *Qualitative Sociology* 6: 212–28.

Lightfoot-Klein, Hanny. 1989. *Prisoners of Ritual: An Odyssey into Female Genital Circumcision in Africa.* New York: Harrington Park Press.

Lukaya, Boniface. 1997. "Wasichana 20 hufariki Dunia kila Mwaka kwa Tohara." *Nipashe* (Dar Es Salaam, Tanzania), 9 September: 7.

Mabala, Richard, and Switbert R. Kamazima. 1995. *The Girl Child in Tan-*

zania: Today's Girl, Tomorrow's Woman: A Research Report. Dar Es Salaam, Tanzania: UNICEF.

Mackie, Gerry. 1996. "Ending Footbinding and Infibulation: A Convention Account." *American Sociological Review* 61: 999–1017.

MacKinnon, Catharine. 1983. "Feminism, Marxism, Method, and the State: Toward Feminist Jurisprudence." In *Feminist Legal Theory,* ed. Katharine Bartlett and Rosanne Kennedy, 181–200. Boulder, Colo.: Westview Press.

March, James G., and Johan P. Olsen. 1998. "The Institutional Dynamics of International Political Orders." *International Organization* 52: 943–69.

Maseke, Lucas. 2001. "Genital Mutilators Threaten to Resume Business." *Guardian* (Dar Es Salaam, Tanzania), April 17.

Matua, Makau. 2001."Savages, Victims, Saviors: The Metaphor of Human Rights." *Harvard International Law Journal* 42: 201–45.

Maurer, Bill. 1997. "Creolization Redux: The Plural Society Thesis and Offshore Financial Services in the British Caribbean." *New West Indies Guide* 71: 249–64.

McAdam, Doug, John D. McCarthy, and Mayer Zald. 1996. "Introduction: Opportunities, Mobilizing Structures, and Framing Processes—Toward a Synthetic, Comparative Perspective on Social Movements." In *Comparative Perspectives on Social Movements: Political Opportunities, Mobilizing Structures, and Cultural Framings,* ed. Doug McAdam, John D. McCarthy, and Mayer Zald, 1–22. Cambridge: Cambridge University Press.

McCann, Hugh, and Dwight Angell. 1993. "House Bill Would Outlaw Female Genital Mutilation." *Detroit News,* November 28: 1C.

McLean, Scilla, and Stella Efua Graham, eds. 1985. *Female Circumcision, Excision, and Infibulation.* 3rd ed. London: Minority Rights Groups.

McNeely, Connie. 1995. *Constructing the Nation-State: International Organization and Prescriptive Action.* Westport, Conn.: Greenwood.

Meinardus, Otto. 1967. "Mythological, Historical, and Sociological Aspects of the Practice of Female Circumcision among Egyptians." *Acta Ethnograhica Academiae Scientaiarum Hungaricae* 17: 387–97.

Merry, Sally Engle. 1995. "Resistance and the Cultural Power of Law," *Law & Society Review* 29: 11–26.

Messing, Simon D. 1980. "The Problem of 'Operations Based on Custom' in Applied Anthropology: The Challenge of the Hosken Report on Genital and Sexual Mutilations of Females." *Human Organization* 39 (1980): 295–97.

Messito, Carol M. 1997–98. "Regulating Rites: Legal Responses to Female Genital Mutilation in the West." *Buffalo Journal of Public Interest Law* 16: 33–77.

Metz, Helen Chapin. 1990. *Egypt: A Country Study.* Washington, D.C.: Federal Research Division, Library of Congress.

Meyer, John W., John Boli, and George M. Thomas. 1987. "Ontology and Rationalization in the Western Cultural Account." In *Institutional Structure: Constituting State, Society, and the Individual,* ed. George M. Thomas, John W. Meyer, Francisco O. Ramirez, and John Boli. Newbury Park, Calif.: Sage.

Meyer, John W., John Boli, George M. Thomas, and Francisco O. Ramirez. 1997. "World Society and the Nation-State." *American Journal of Sociology* 103: 144–81.

Meyer, John W., and Ronald L. Jepperson. 2000. "The 'Actors' of Modern Society: The Cultural Construction of Social Agency." *Sociological Theory* 18: 100–20.

Mohanty, Chandra Talpade. 1991. "Introduction: Cartographies of Struggle: Third World Women and the Politics of Feminism." In *Third World Women and the Politics of Feminism,* ed. Chandra Talpade Mohanty, Ann Russo, and Lourdes Torres. Bloomington, Ind.: Indiana University Press.

Moustafa, Tamir. 2000. "Conflict and Cooperation between the State and Religious Institutions in Contemporary Egypt." *International Journal of Middle East Studies* 32: 3–22.

Murray, Jocelyn Margaret. 1976. "Church Missionary Society and the Female Circumcision." *Journal of Religion in Africa* 8: 92–104.

Narayan, Uma. 1997. *Dislocating Cultures: Identities, Traditions, and Third-World Feminism.* New York: Routledge.

National Council for Population and Development, Central Bureau of Statistics (Office of the Vice President and Ministry of Planning and National Development [Kenya]), and Macro International. 1999. *Kenya Demographic and Health Surveys 1998.* Calverton, Md.

Natsoulas, Theodore. 1998. "The Politicization of the Ban on Female Circumcision and the Rise of the Independent School Movement in Kenya: The KCA, the Missions and Government, 1929–1932." *JAAS* 33: 137–58.

Nkoma-Wamunza, A. G., Kakuru Katalyeba, Peter C. T. Mayeye, and Anna Mwasha. 1998. *The Study of Women and Girls in Tanzania: A Study on Knowledge, Attitudes, and Practices with a Gender Perspective in Twelve Selected Districts.* Dar Es Salaam, Tanzania: UNICEF.

Obermeyer, Carla Makhlouf. 1999. "Female Genital Surgeries: The Known, the Unknown, and the Unknowable." *Medical Anthropology Quarterly* 13: 79–106.

Obiora, L. Amede. 1997. "Bridges and Barricades: Rethinking Polemics and Intransigence in the Campaign against Female Circumcision." *Case Western Reserve Law Review* 47: 275–377.

Onuf, Nicholas. 1995. "Intervention for the Common Good." In *Beyond Westphalia? State Sovereignty and International Intervention*, ed. G. Lyons and M. Mastanduno, 45–58. Baltimore: Johns Hopkins University Press.

Parker, Melissa. 1995. "Rethinking Female Circumcision." *Africa* 65: 506–24.

PATH/MYWO. 1998. *Circumcision with Words: Fighting FGM in Kenya: A Project Implemented by the Program for Appropriate Technology and Health (PATH) and Maendeleo Ya Wanawake Organization (MYWO)*.

Pedriana, Nicholas, and Robin Stryker. 1997. "Political Culture Wars 1960s Style: Equal Employment Opportunity-Affirmative Action Law and the Philadelphia Plan." *American Journal of Sociology* 103: 633–91.

Peters, Julie, and Andrea Wolper, eds. 1995. *Women's Rights, Human Rights: International Feminist Perspectives*. New York: Routledge.

Powell, Walter, and Paul DiMaggio, eds. 1991. *The New Institutionalism in Organizational Analysis*. Chicago: University of Chicago Press.

Preves, Sharon. 1999. *Sexing the Intersexed: Lived Experiences in Socio-Cultural Context*. Ph.D. diss., University of Minnesota.

Price, Richard M. 1997. *The Chemical Weapons Taboo*. Ithaca, N.Y.: Cornell University Press.

Rahman, Anika, and Nahid Toubia, eds. 2000. *Female Genital Mutilation: A Guide to Laws and Policies Worldwide*. London: Zed Books.

Ramirez, Francisco O., and John Boli. 1987. "Global Patterns of Educational Institutionalism." In *Institutional Structure: Constituting State, Society, and the Individual*, ed. George M. Thomas, John W. Meyer, Francisco O. Ramirez, and John Boli, 150–72. Newbury Park, Calif.: Sage.

Ramirez, Francisco O., and Elizabeth McEneaney. 1997. "From Women's Suffrage to Reproduction Rights?" *International Journal of Comparative Sociology* 38: 6–24.

Ramirez, Francisco O., Yasemin Soysal, and Suzanne Shanahan. 1997. "The Changing Logic of Political Citizenship: Cross-National Acquisition of Women's Suffrage Rights, 1890–1990." *American Sociological Review* 62: 735–45.

Risse, Thomas, and Kathryn Sikkink. 1999. "The Socialization of International Human Rights Norms into Domestic Politics." In *The Power of Human Rights: International Norms and Domestic Change*, ed. Thomas Risse, Stephen C. Ropp, and Kathryn Sikkink, 1–38. Cambridge: Cambridge University Press.

Robertson, Claire. 1996. "Grassroots in Kenya: Women, Genital Mutiliation, and Collective Action, 1920–1990." *Signs* 21: 615–42.

Robertson, Roland. 1995. "Globalization: Time-Space and Homogeneity-

Heterogeneity." In *Global Modernities,* ed. Mike Featherstone, Scott Lash, and Roland Robertson, 25–44. London: Sage Publications.

Rosberg, Carl, and Robert Jackson. 1982. "Why Africa's Weak States Persist: The Empirical and Juridical in Statehood." *World Politics* 35: 1–24.

Ruggie, John Gerard. 1993. "Territoriality and Beyond: Problematizing Modernity in International Relations." *International Organizations* 47: 139–74.

Said, Edward. 1993. *Culture and Imperialism.* New York: Knopf.

Seif El Dawla, Aida. 1999. "The Political and Legal Struggle over Female Genital Mutilation in Egypt: Five Years since the ICPD." *Reproductive Health Matters* 7: 128–36.

Shandall, A. A. 1967. "Circumcision and Infibulation of Females: A General Consideration of the Problem and a Clinical Study of the Complications in Sudanese Women." *Sudan Medical Journal* 5: 178–212.

Shweder, Richard A., Hazel R. Markus, Martha L. Minow, and Frank Kessel. 1997. "The Free Exercise of Culture: Ethnic Customs, Assimilation and American Law." *Items* 51: 61–67.

Silbey, Susan. 1997. "Let Them Eat Cake": Globalization, Postmodernism, Colonialism, and the Possibilities of Justice." *Law and Society Review* 31: 207–35.

Simms, Shelley. 1993. "What's Culture Got to Do with It? Excising the Harmful Tradition of Female Circumcision." *Harvard Law Review* 106: 1944–61.

Slack, Alice T. 1988. "Female Circumcision: A Critical Appraisal." *Human Rights Quarterly* 10: 437–86.

Smith, Jaqueline. 1995. *Visions and Discussions on Genital Mutilation of Girls: An International Survey.* Amsterdam: Defense for Children International.

Smith, Robin Cerny. 1992. "Female Circumcision: Bringing Women's Perspectives into the International Debate." *Southern California Law Review* 65: 2449–504.

Snow, David A., and Robert D. Benford. 1992. "Master Frames and Cycles of Protest." In *Frontiers in Social Movement Theory,* ed. Aldon Morris and Carol McClurg Mueller, 133–54. New Haven: Yale.

Soysal, Yasemin N. 1994. *Limits of Citizenship: Migrants and Postnational Membership in Europe.* Chicago: University of Chicago Press.

Stetson, Dorothy McBride. 1995. "Human Rights for Women: International Compliance with a Feminist Standard." *Women & Politics* 15: 71–95.

Stevens, Guy H. 1996. "Translating Human Rights into Women's Rights." *Peace Review* 8: 411–15.

Sudan Demographic and Health Survey. 1989–90. Department of Statistics, Ministry of Economic & National Planning.

Sussman, Erika. 1998. "Contending with Culture: An Analysis of the Female Genital Mutilation Act of 1996." *Cornell International Law Journal* 31: 101.

Swart, William J. 1995. "The League of Nations and the Irish Question: Master Frames, Cycles of Protest, and 'Master Frame Alignment.'" *Sociological Quarterly* 36: 465–81.

Tanaka, Kiyofumi. 2000. *Medical Anthropological Study in Western Kenya and Its Implications for Community Health Development.* Report of the International Development Center of Japan.

Temba, Pudenciana. 1997. "Uncalled for Deaths: FGM Mortality High in Tarime." *Sunday News* (Dar Es Salaam, Tanzania), October 19: 1.

Thomas, George M., and John W. Meyer. 1984. "The Expansion of the State." *Annual Review of Sociology* 10: 461–82.

Toubia, Nahid. 1994. "Female Genital Mutilation and the Responsibility of Reproductive Health Professionals." *International Journal of Gynecology & Obstetrics* 46: 127–35.

———. 1995. *A Call for Global Action.* New York: RAINBO.

Toubia, Nahid, and S. Izett. 1998. *Female Genital Mutilation: An Overview.* Geneva, Switzerland: World Health Organization.

UNICEF. 1996. *A Strategic Framework and Programming Guidelines to Eliminate Female Genital Mutilation.* New York.

United Nations. 1959. *United Nations Yearbook.*

———. 1963. General Assembly Official Records, 18th Session, Supplement No. 15, A/5515 9/17–12/17.

———. 1982. *United Nations Yearbook.*

United Nations. 1983. *Committee on the Elimination of Discrimination against Women (CEDAW), Second Session; Consideration of Reports Submitted by States Parties under Article 18 of the Convention; Initial Reports of States Parties: Arab Republic of Egypt.* CEDAW/C/5/Add.10, 3 February.

United Nations. 1987. *Committee on the Elimination of Discrimination against Women (CEDAW); Consideration of Reports Submitted by States Parties under Article 18 of the Convention; Second Periodic Report of States Parties; Addendum: Egypt.* CEDAW/C/13/Add.2, 14 May.

United Nations. 1989. *Committee on the Elimination of Discrimination against Women (CEDAW); Consideration of Reports Submitted by States Parties under Article 18 of the Convention; Second Periodic Report of States Parties; Addendum: Arab Republic of Egypt.* CEDAW/C/13/Add.2/Amend.1, 4 December.

United Nations. 1990. *Report of the Committee on the Elimination of Discrimination against Women, Ninth Session.* General Assembly Official Records, 45th Session, Supplement No. 38, A/45/38.

United Nations. 1996. *Committee on the Elimination of Discrimination against Women (CEDAW); Consideration of Reports Submitted by States Parties under*

Article 18 of the Convention; Third Periodic Reports of States Parties: Egypt. CEDAW/C/EGY/3, 25 July.

United Nations. 1999. *Committee on the Rights of the Child; Consideration of Reports Submitted by States Parties under Article 44 of the Convention; Periodic Reports of States Parties Due in 1997; Addendum: Egypt.* CRC/C/65/Add.9, 11 November.

United Republic of Tanzania. 1999. *National Female Genital Mutilation (FGM) Conference, Dodoma, 16th November 1999: Report.* Dodoma, Tanzania: Ministry of Community Development, Women Affairs and Children (MCDWAC).

United Republic of Tanzania, Ministry of Finance. 1997–98. *Annual Report on Debt Management in Tanzania.* Dar Es Salaam, Tanzania: Accountant General's Department.

U.S. Central Intelligence Agency. 1999. *World Factbook.* 1 January. www.cia. gov/cia/publications/factbook/index.html.

U.S. Department of Justice, Immigration and Naturalization Service. 1995. *1995 Statistical Yearbook of the Immigration and Naturalization Service.*

U.S. Department of State. 1996. *Country Reports on Human Rights Practices for 1996: Africa.* www.state.gov/www/global/human_rights/96hrp_index. html.

U.S. Department of State. 1997. *Country Reports on Human Rights Practices for 1997: Africa.* www.state.gov/www/global/human_rights/97hrp_index. html.

U.S. Department of State. 1998. *Country Reports on Human Rights Practices for 1998: Africa.* www.state.gov/www/global/human_rights/98hrp_index. html.

U.S. Department of State. 1999. *Country Reports on Human Rights Practices for 1999: Africa.* www.state.gov/g/drl/rls/hrrpt/1999/.

U.S. Department of State. 2000. *Country Reports on Human Rights Practices for 2000: Africa.* www.state.gov/g/drl/rls/hrrpt/2000/.

Villagelife Panorama Projects. 2001. "Campaign for the Eradication of Female Genital Mutilation (FGM)—The Human Scourge." Letter to the author, 31 May.

Wada, Shohei. 1992. "Changes in the Practice of FGM among the Iraqw in Tanzania." *Senri Ethnological Studies* 4: 159–72.

Walker, Alice. 1992. *Possessing the Secret of Joy.* New York: Harcourt Brace.

Walker, Alice, and Pratibha Parmar. 1993. *Warrior Marks: Female Genital Mutilation and the Sexual Blinding of Women.* New York: Harcourt Brace.

Walley, Christine J. 1997. "Searching for 'Voices': Feminism, Anthropology, and the Global Debate over Female Genital Operations." *Cultural Anthropology* 12: 405–38.

Warren, Priscilla. 1994. "Women are Human: Gender-Based Persecution Is a Human Rights Violation against Women." *Hastings Women's Law Journal* 5: 281–315.

Waters, Malcolm. 1995. *Globalization.* London: Routledge.

———. 1996. "Human Rights and the Universalisation of Interests: Towards a Social Constructionist Approach." *Sociology* 30: 593–600.

Weinstein, Wareen. 1983. "Human Rights and Development in Africa: Dilemmas and Options." *Daedalus* 112: 171–96.

Williams, Lindy, and Teresa Sobieszczyk. 1997. "Attitudes Surrounding the Continuation of Female Circumcision in the Sudan: Passing the Tradition to the Next Generation." *Journal of Marriage and the Family* 59: 966–81.

Winter, Bronwyn. 1994. "Women, the Law, and Cultural Relativism in France." *Signs: Journal of Women in Culture and Society* 19: 939–74.

World Bank. 2000. *World Development Indicators.* Washington, D.C.

World Health Organization. 1997. Female Genital Mutilation. Fact Sheet No. 153. April.

World Health Organization/UNICEF/UN Family Planning Association/ United Nations Development Program. 1995. *Joint Statement on Female Genital Mutilation.* First draft.

Worsley, Allan. 1967. "Infibulation and Female Circumcision: A Study of a Little Known Custom." *British Journal of Obstetrics and Gynaecology* 45: 686–91.

INDEX

· ·